Why You Are Alive On Earth

Why do You Exist?

V. G. Blanchette Jr

Revision 2 2005031

ISBN: 0692800441
ISBN-13: 978-0692800447

PREFACE

Recently a beautiful fourteen-year-old Junior High School student with her whole life ahead of her came home, entered her bedroom, and hung herself. Why?

A mother of three small children loaded them in the car and drove into the ocean in an apparent attempt to drown them. Why?

Thousands of people, including both teenagers and adults of all ages, consume harmful substances such as cocaine and heroin, smoke cigarettes, and drink excessive amounts of alcohol. Why?

Often these kinds of destructive acts happen because the individual feels life has no purpose or is meaningless. They may see life as a struggle and feel their lives have little value. Their actions reveal they don't know who they really are and what their true value is.

Some people don't know why they are alive. Could that be you? Are you living like a mouse that has been dropped into a big, complicated maze? Do you wander around, lost, trying this turn and that turn, doing what we see others doing, bumping into walls, and getting no closer to the cheese at the end of the maze? You might not even know there is something wonderful waiting for you at the end of the maze.

Public domain image by Arek Socha from Pixabay

Lost people need a model of the maze that gives them a birds-eye view so that they can see the path through life to the prize at the end.

This book provides that model, and reveals "**Why you are alive on Earth.**" It will help you through the maze by revealing the two major illusions many of us are trapped in. It will also help you bring your personality into harmony with the One who created you. With that knowledge you will find joy, peace and a new awe of the world around you and the wonderful future ahead of you.

Contents

Introduction

It is quite normal for us to wonder why we are alive. We all know the human body eventually dies, and the person expressed by that body seems to be gone. Was that person really there? Does he or she still exist somewhere after their body lies in the grave? Or was what we thought to be a person just the electrical activity in that person's brain?

It's natural for us to ask these kinds of questions after seeing the death of someone we love. Our heart yearns to know our loved one is safe, and that we will see them again, but the answers science gives us are rather dark and hopeless. Why? Because science deals with the physical world, and none of our senses (taste, touch, smell, hearing, or sight) can detect or measure the presence of the person we now miss. If we allow for continued-life of the person after the body dies, then there has to be something else happening other than brain activity. There has to be a process beyond ordinary science. This book explores that idea and provides a "model" for understanding that process.

The model developed within this book is not absolute truth because only God, the creator of the universe, knows what actually exists and how it all works. However, this model does help us understand who we are, why we are alive on Earth, what death really means, and what we can expect when we die.

In fact, there is evidence that the person continues to exist after the body dies, and we will explore this via the bible and eyewitness accounts.

The human body lives only in the natural world, otherwise known as the physical universe or, in scientific circles, the space-time continuum. You may believe that the natural world is all there is or ever will be (reminiscent of the thoughts of Carl Sagan, an American astronomer, cosmologist, astrophysicist, and author). But keep in mind that there was a time when the scientific community, the wisest men of their day, believed the Earth was flat and the sun circled the Earth. Actually, the argument that "the natural world is all there is or will ever be" is really a religious belief that a Creator does not exist. This belief is religious because it is scientifically unproven yet accepted by faith. Using a logical extension of this argument (that the natural world is all there is or will ever be), scientists conclude that the entire universe must have appeared out of absolutely nothing all by itself. If this is your present belief, then you are invited to suspend your belief for a few hours while you read this book. The author believes that what you'll find here will stimulate your thinking on the subject of the continuation of life after death.

This book will tell you what the Creator revealed about how and why He is creating humans, and what you can expect to happen to you when your body dies.[1] This book will attempt to free you from the deadly illusion in which many people are living.

[1] In this book the King James Version (KJV) of the Bible is used. The author has lightly and selectively paraphrased some quoted Scripture to bring it closer to modern English without modifying the meaning, and to enrich its meaning using Strong's Concordance as pertaining to the central subject of this book.

1 The First Great Illusion

As you look through your eyes and listen through your ears, where is the real you, the "you" who is doing this looking and hearing? Most people feel they are at the center of their heads. This strong illusion exists because our hearing is binaural, and because we see in stereo vision.

The illusion we all live in is that we are in our body's head. You feel this must be true because your eyes are on the front of your head, and your ears are at that same level above the ground, so it is natural to perceive yourself as located at that level between your ears and right behind your eyes where your brain sits. You have probably been taught that the electrical activity in your brain makes you who you are. Thus you live with the powerful mental illusion that you are your brain.

You are actually not your brain. There is self-imposed misconception going on here. To understand this, consider the example of an illusion called a mirage. You may have seen a mirage. The most common mirage is when you look far down a long highway on a hot summer day and see what looks like a lake sitting where the road should be. However, if you drive to that distant lake you will find no water there. In fact, nothing is there except the road.

Scientists tell us the "water" in this type of mirage is an illusion caused by the way the hot air above the road's surface bends the light from the blue sky. What looks like water is really just light from the blue sky refracted by a layer of hot air and directed towards you.

People struggling through the hot, dry desert have been deceived by a mirage lake and have died trying to reach its nonexistent water. An example of this is the eighty-seven families of the Montgomery wagon train and hundreds of their animals which perished in the western USA in the 1800s due to the deception of a mirage.[2] This loss of life demonstrates that powerful illusions can harm us if we are not careful, if we are not aware of illusions, and if we do not use our minds to think through to the truth.

---

[2] An account of the loss of the Montgomery wagon train can be found on page 77 of the book *Struggles for Life and Home in the North-West* by Geo. W. France, New York: I. Goldmann, Steam Printer, 7, 9, & 11, New Chambers St. 1890.

> Powerful illusions can harm us if we are not aware of them, and if we do not use our minds to think through to the truth.

Using our minds, we can see that our perceptions of where we are would change if our eyes and ears were down on our ankles. (This is silly, but just go along with this idea for a moment.) Imagine you had been born with your eyes and ears on your left and right ankles. (Assume you are not wearing socks.) Your left eye and ear on your left ankle and your right eye and ear on your right ankle would be feeding sensory input up nerve pathways to your brain where the images would be combined to give you stereoscopic vison and stereo hearing. The stereo nature of vision and hearing would cause you to perceive your location as centered between your left and right ankles, just as you now sense you are inside your head between your ears. This would be a very strange sensation.

What makes this illusion so striking is that at the location you would perceive yourself to be there is no physical part of your body. You would be receiving sensory images and sounds that seem to come from a place *between your ankles.* Your perception would be that you are in the air where no part of your body exists. If a cat walked between your legs, you would get the mysterious sensation that it had walked right through you!

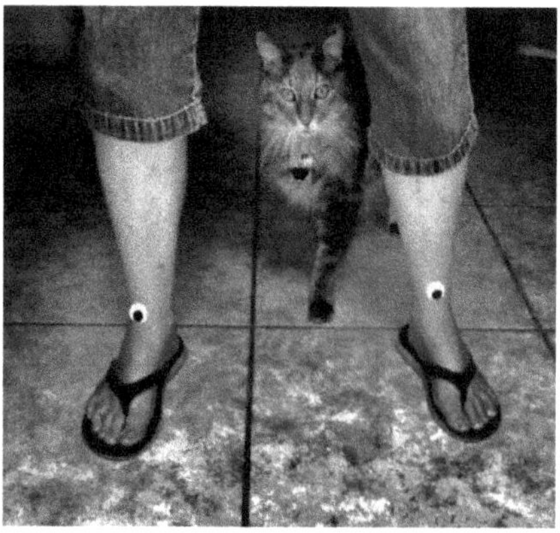

The realization that we would perceive our location to be in the space between our ankles and near the floor, where no part of our physical body exists, is another clue that our perception that we are in our body's head is just a powerful illusion.

The idea that you are in your head is a formidable illusion. It began operating on you in your mother's womb when you first heard sounds. It became stronger when you were born and your eyes began to see the world around you, and stronger still when you began tasting foods that came into your mouth. As the years have passed you have become comfortable being you in your head.

Likewise, the longer you see that wonderful patch of clear, blue water out there on the dessert's horizon, the more convinced you are that it is real and that if you hiked out there you could get a refreshing drink. After all, *it's been there all your life.* Likewise you have believed you are your head and brain all your life. You have just believed it and never questioned it.

What if I told you that you are not your head and brain? What if I said... *You have been deceived by an illusion as dangerous as the one that killed every living person and animal on the Montgomery wagon train?*

Think about this; we would have a hard time convincing the wagon master that the water he thinks he sees is not real. Why? Because he is sure he sees it. He trusts his eyes. The illusion is so strong it will kill him. The illusion you believe about being your brain can kill you too.

Now, if you will consider a little dirt, and truth revealed through Scripture, you will be able to see that you are not in your head.[3]

---

[3] It is impossible for you or me to know anything about who we really are, where we are really located, and what we were created for, using only our five senses because they are confined within the natural world's space-time continuum. We can still answer these questions, however, because the Creator, the One who made the natural world and ourselves, has revealed the answers to these questions.

2 The Formation of a Person

The Nature of Dirt

You know dirt. When it clings together you call the clumps clods and when it is about the size of sugar, you might call it sand. If it is made of very small particles you can blow away with your breath, you call it dust. You have held it, swept it up, maybe washed it off a dirty car, and, as a baby, you probably ate some of it. But what exactly is it? *This is important because the Bible says your body is made of dust.*[4]

> **7 And the LORD God formed man of the dust of the ground, and breathed into his nostrils the breath of life; and man became a living soul.**
>
> **Genesis 2:7**

Notice this is not some special dust. This "dust of the ground" is earth dirt, nothing more and nothing less. What is this dust made of?

Scientists say this "dust," and all the solid, liquid, and gaseous materials we see, feel, and touch, are made of tiny particles they have named atoms. Oddly enough, scientists also tell us that atoms are not really solid particles. They have found that atoms are actually empty space containing concentrated electric and nuclear force fields, and there is absolutely nothing solid there, even though they feel solid when we bump into a wall or close a car door on our finger. They tell us that atoms are made of these force "fields" and consist of mostly empty space. The "hardness" or "solid" appearance of materials is just another illusion.

Consider also what space is made of. The electric fields and nuclear forces of atoms exist in space, but what exactly is "space"? Some may argue that space is just emptiness (i.e., a location where there is nothing). But space is not just "nothing" because it can be measured and a volume of

---

[4] The Bible contains more than 4,000 years of wisdom written by men but believed to be revealed to mankind from some "outside source." Most folks who bother to read and study the Bible consider it to be **B**asic **I**nstructions **B**efore **L**eaving **E**arth.

space can be determined. You cannot measure "nothing," so space is something and therefore *just as "created" as electric and nuclear forces.* No one knows how space was made or what space is made of.

Do you realize what is being said here? Not only are you not in your head, your body is made of dust (atoms), electric "fields" and nuclear "forces" you think of as solid matter. On top of that, the rest of your body that is not electric fields and nuclear forces is just space; an emptiness that is something that has been created.

This idea that empty space is a created thing is difficult for some people to grasp. It might help to think of it this way: if you could find a place where there was *absolutely nothing* there would be no empty space there either. The universe we live in was created from *absolutely nothing.*

Can you see that the world we exist in is just one illusion upon another?

> **Not only are you not in your head, your body is made of electric "fields" and nuclear "forces," not solid matter. The fact that you believe it's solid matter is just another illusion.**

The Formation of a Person

This dust the Bible talks about is made up of atoms and molecules, so how can it form a person? What a fantastic question!

Someone may argue that we are not just made of dust, but that we are made of organic molecules, DNA,[5] blood, and many other highly complex biological assemblies. If you hear this, remember that organic molecules, DNA, blood, and everything else in our bodies are made of atoms - the basic "dust" of our world. You cannot get beyond the fact that as complex and wonderfully made as our bodies are, the human body and all its parts down to the cellular level (and parts inside the cell) are made of atoms, the basic particulate "dust" of the Earth.

This is why in this book we will sometimes refer to your human body

---

[5] DNA is DeoxyriboNucleic Acid, a material that can replicate itself which is present in nearly all living organisms as the main constituent of chromosomes. It is the carrier of the instructions that create human bodies.

as your dust-body or Earth-suit to constantly remind you that your body is nothing but empty space, electric fields, and nuclear force fields.

But atoms, molecules, blood, DNA, and even the most complex organic molecules cannot utter a single word. They cannot love; they cannot speak; they cannot desire. They simply make up parts that combine to make a **chemical life form we call a human body.** The human body is a very complex, self-sustaining, chemical reaction maintained by energy exchanges in the body's cells and ultimately expressed in cellular reproduction for repair and growth. The human body uses energy from food (chiefly sugar molecules - another form of dust) to animate itself and keep its chemical processes going. Eventually this complex, ongoing chemical reaction fails, all the body's processes stop working, and the body disintegrates back into inanimate dust. This is the dust the Bible is speaking about in this passage:

> **19 You shall work and it's by the sweat of your brow you shall eat bread, up until the day you return unto the ground; for out of the ground you were taken: for you are dust, and unto dust you shall return.[6]**
>
> **Genesis 3:19**

Look at it this way: sperm meets the egg at the instant of conception of a baby and this wonderfully complex chemical reaction starts and continues, eventually growing into a new human body. Its growth follows the detailed instructions in the very first cell's DNA.[7] But the body is just a chemical reaction that can be stopped by simply adding too much salt (as an abortionist may do to kill a baby in the womb), or stopped by shutting off oxygen for five minutes, or stopped by various diseases or physical

---

[6] Why didn't the writer of Genesis use "atoms" instead of "dust"? When Genesis was written, common people knew nothing of atoms, molecules, and force fields. The words used expressed truth in the clearest way possible for the knowledge of that day (i.e., the human body is really made of "dust," and when it dies it returns to inanimate dirt).

[7] Researchers are still learning about the complexity of DNA, but one thing is clear, and becoming clearer as more is known: the Human Genome (DNA) could not possibly have evolved from some pool of warm water and minerals over billions of years because it is irreducibly complex. *The information coded into the DNA is itself a created thing.*

damage caused by an accident.

But here is an interesting puzzle: observation tells us that every human body eventually dies, and we observe that when this happens nothing remains of the "person". The body decays back into dust and the person no longer communicates with us. Yet the Bible tells us people can live forever. If this Bible claim is true, it should be obvious to you that the body (a chemical reaction) cannot possibly be a person.

An ongoing chemical reaction can look like a living person, but that is not real life because when the body dies nothing remains but dust. If you argue the body is the person, then you have to conclude that the person you knew cannot continue to exist because the body returns to dust.

Was the appearance of a person just another illusion? Is the Bible wrong? After all, it says, "The LORD God formed man of the dust of the ground."

No, it's not wrong. Look carefully at what the Bible says God did. This time we will use the actual Hebrew meaning of what the King James Bible scholars translated as "breath."

> **7 "And the LORD God formed man of the dust of the ground, and breathed into his nostrils *the spirit of life*; and man became a living soul."[8]**
>
> **Genesis 2:7**

Notice three things:

1. Genesis 2:7 says that God formed your body from "dust of the ground." In modern language this means that atoms in the food your mother ate passed into her bloodstream, through the placenta, and into your baby-body's bloodstream. These atoms (earth dust) were then used by the ongoing chemical reactions in your cells to allow the cells of your body to grow and multiply.

2. Something has been added to the body made of dust. The Creator gave your body the "spirit of life". *He breathed you into your body.*

---

[8] From *Strong's Concordance.* Breath 5397: wind, angry or vital breath, divine inspiration, intellect, an animal blast that breathed inspiration, soul, spirit.

3. The word *breath* is the Hebrew word נְשָׁמָה which means "a divinely inspired spirit." Thus Genesis 2:7 is saying that God gave the dust, the baby's body shaped like you, a spirit that has life and you became a living soul. ***Life is the spirit, not in the miraculous arrangement of the atoms that make up the body***.

The Bible did not say God made a living pile of dust, but instead he used the human-body-shaped atoms and molecules to be connected with the real you (the Spirit you). He calls YOU a living soul. Your spirit is the *true you* that looks into nature and manipulates things in the natural world through your physical body, which God designed. This concept is reinforced by what the Bible says happens to the human body when a person dies. This passage is from Ecclesiastes 12:7.

7 Then shall the dust return to the earth as it was: and the spirit shall return unto God who gave it.

This clearly shows that the body returns as dust to the earth, taking with it its entire DNA. It can do nothing else because the body is only dust (atoms and molecules, which are mostly just empty space). The exciting part is that the spirit God breathed into the dust returns to Him! Death of the body does not destroy the spirit. We will see this truly is *life-changing information.*

Now reread what we just went over until your mind finally sees through the powerful illusion that you are just a body.

You think you are your body. This false concept is the mirage, the dangerous illusion. Why? Because you are not your body. You are actually a spirit inhabiting your physical body and you (a spirit) looks out through the body's eyes, which, as the poets say, are the windows to the soul.

A chemical reaction cannot be a person.

The life that is YOU is spirit, not dust or molecules. Your spirit uses the body's senses (sight, sound, touch, taste, and smell) to live in and experience the natural world. You can think of the human body as a portal for a human spirit to participate in the natural world.

This should be a comfortable concept to grasp if you are a computer gamer. It is now possible to buy special helmets that encase the game player's head and provide both sound and visual scenes. This helmet immerses the player in whatever universe the computer generates in three-dimensional moving pictures and stereo sound. With the helmet on, you could be looking at the surface of Mars with visions of rust-colored sand and listening to the faint whistling of Martian wind, or you could be looking at a jungle ruin deep in the Amazon basin and hearing the sounds of jungle animals and native drums. These deeply immersive experiences can give you the sensation that you are actually on Mars or deep in the Amazon jungle. Other players wearing their own helmets and connected to their own computers can join you in the game via the internet . In those artificial worlds you see and interact with other players.

And, in fact, that is exactly where you are - you are a player in God's game of life which is serious and real. In this "game" you don't have to wear a helmet because you are inside your physical body with all of its sights, sounds, and sensations being fed to you, a spirit. You are a spirit, not a body. Look around you and you will see others who are in this extravagant, fantastic, unbelievable, *instructional illusion* we call being alive on Earth.

Some of you reading this may have seen the 1999 science fiction movie "The Matrix" where the hacker Neo discovers a powerful computer has subjugated the entire human race. All the subjugated humans are attached to the computer and spend their entire lives sleeping in capsules while the computer keeps their bodies alive and harvests their mental energy. What they think is the real world is nothing but a dream-state. A team of renegades (free humans) struggle with this computer to free other people and bring them back to the real world. They free the protagonist Neo and the plot continues from there.

What you really are and where you live is far beyond the ideas presented in "The Matrix." You live in the illusion that you are a physical body that came out of your mother's womb and that you walk around in the natural world until one day your body dies and that is the end of you. But this is not the truth. You are a spirit that uses the human body as a portal into the natural world, and there is no computer running the show.[9]

This can be an extraordinary concept to connect with - to realize you are not what you see in the mirror. It is exciting to discover this truth and throw off the illusion you are only the body you see.

You can think of the human body as a portal for a human spirit to participate in the natural world.

Try this experiment. The next time you are with a group of people, use your mind to think of each of those people as bodies made of dust, just complex chemical reactions, each in his or her individual shape. Then think of the actual persons inside those "Earth-suits" as spirits. Look at someone, John, for example, and think *there is a spirit named John inside that body made of atoms.* Watch as that spirit-person (soul) moves its Earth-suit; watch as it talks and communicates the spirit-John's feelings with facial expressions and gestures of the hands and arms. Try it, thinking only that a person's spirit *inside* that body is making it move. At some point you should start to get the odd sensation that the world is not so predictable any longer. It becomes strange and wonderful at the same time.

A sense of amazement may come over you. In a sense, you have taken Morpheus' red pill.[10] When that happens, your mind has broken through the powerful illusion that has been controlling you since you were born, and you are starting to realize the truth about where you really are and who you really are.

---

9 We will talk about who is running the show, and you will discover He is not only wonderful but has your best interest in mind. You were created to know Him and be in loving relationship with Him forever.

10 A reference to a scene in the movie "The Matrix" where the hacker Neo is given the choice between taking the blue pill or the red pill. If he chooses the blue pill, his memory of the contact with true reality (the free humans) will be erased and he will live out his life in the computer-controlled Matrix, ignorant of the truth. If he takes the red pill, Morpheus tells him "… you stay in wonderland and I show you how deep the rabbit hole goes." In other words, Neo will begin to see truth clearer and clearer, and it will astound him. If you can tolerate a lot of shoot-em-up type violence, this is a great sci-fi movie. Check it out.

But wait; there are more exciting things for you to find out about yourself. Huge implications flow out of the fact that people are spirits and not just dust-bodies. *You are much more than you think.*

Does all this sound a little wacky to you? If so, consider the thirsty man who has just pointed at the distant mirage lake out in the desert and has told you he is betting his life on hiking out there to reach the water. You say to him,

"Don't go. That is a mirage; there is no water there."

He answers, "You're crazy; I can see the water shimmering in the distance. I can see it with my own eyes so I know it is there. I am thirsty and I am going."

He is totally fooled by the illusion, and *he will die believing it*, even though you are speaking truth to him. ***His belief in what his eyes tell him will kill him***, but you are safe from going after that illusion of water because your belief is different from his; your mind holds a belief based on truth. ***This demonstrates that what you believe, or don't believe, can kill you.*** On the other hand, knowing the truth can protect you from harm. That is precisely why you need to read the rest of this book, for there is real danger in living out your entire life blinded by the illusion you are nothing but a body.

What you believe, or don't believe, can kill you. Knowing the truth can protect you from harm.

Wouldn't it have been nice if the Creator had just given us more details about where we are, who we really are, and why we were created? On second thought, He did give us this information. Perhaps the problem is not His communication skills, but that we humans have never bothered to study the Basic Instructions before Leaving Earth (B.I.B.L.E.) with an open and inquiring mind. Let's dig a little deeper in the next chapter as we investigate "What does it really mean to be born?"

3 What it Really Means to be Born

Consider this beautiful passage from Psalms:

> **13 For God You have possessed my reins: You have covered me in my mother's womb.**
> **14 I will praise You; for I am fearfully and wonderfully made: marvelous are Your works; and that my soul knows this for sure.**
> **15 My substance was not hidden from You, when I was made in secret, and curiously wrought in the lowest parts of the Earth.**
> **16 Your eyes did see my substance yet being unperfect; and in Your book all my members were written, which in continuance were fashioned, when as yet there was none of them.**
> **Psalm 139:13-16**

The above passage describes God's creation of a human being in the womb. The language is the King James English from hundreds of years ago, and it is not easy to understand. Let's take a second look at this passage, substituting enriched meaning found in the original Hebrew words. Words enclosed in parenthesis are the author's additional interpretive explanation.

> **13 For God You have procured and erected my mind: You have knit me together in my mother's womb.**
> **14 I will praise You; for I am fearfully and wonderfully made: marvelous are Your works; and that my soul knows this for sure.**
> **15 My strength and energy were not hidden from You, when I was made in secret, and fabricated as in embroidering or needlework, in fine detail and rich complexity in the lowest (smallest) parts of the**

solid material (soil; i.e., atoms).[11]
16 Your eyes did see my substance before it was formed; and in Your book all my pieces were prescribed, which were set to be fashioned in a sequenced flow of time, when as yet there was none of them. **Psalm 139:13-16**

Notice that verse 13 says God "...knit me together in my mother's womb." Many people think this sentence describes God making a baby's body in the womb; however, because of recent scientific discoveries about the growth of a baby in the womb, we now know this Scripture cannot be talking about the baby's body. Why? Well remember that all baby bodies are made of dust (atoms and molecules). Science has shown us that the baby gradually grows from just one cell into a fully formed human baby made of billions of cells. The baby's body does not form different parts like the teeth, the heart, the liver, and legs, and then when they are each fully formed somehow God knits them together into a whole baby whose parts work together correctly. What actually happens is the tiny cells in the growing baby (embryo) *differentiate gradually*. This means as the cells divide, the two cells formed by each division are slightly different from each other, guided by the DNA instructions in the cell nucleus. As this division happens over and over again, the cells form clusters of cells, which are ever more distinct in function, with some cell clusters eventually becoming hair; others teeth; and others hearts, lungs, livers, and legs as the cells multiply. It is an ongoing, constant, gradual process all throughout the mass of cells growing in the mother's womb.

What God did was make a place for the cells of a baby to grow (the womb), and made the very first cell of the baby contain the complete instructions to direct how all of the baby-body cells are to differentiate as they multiply (***set to be fashioned in a sequenced flow of time – Psalm 139:16***). The instructions are in the DNA of the first cell, and are so wonderfully complex and complete that at the right time each of the ever

---

[11] Verse 15 mentions "lowest parts" and "solid material," which does not make sense, but at that time long ago, before the knowledge of atoms and molecules existed, this was the best explanation God could give and have hope that the writer of Psalms could begin to understand. God knew that mankind would one day correctly understand what He put in simple terms long ago. He has knitted our spirits into our dust-bodies at the atomic level or deeper.

larger number of cells gradually differentiate into the whole, complex mass of cells we call a human baby, with all its parts complete. God does not have to knit any of the baby's body parts together because its parts form continuously from beginning to the end. When it is done, it is finished, with a fully functioning little human body with no seams or stitches.

God does not have to knit any of the baby's body parts together because its parts form continuously from beginning to the end.

God set up birth to be automatic once the first cell begins multiplying and growing until the baby is ready to be born. God doesn't need to intervene. His DNA code and chemical reactions do all that is necessary to form a viable baby body. (That in itself is pretty amazing.) Does this mean the Scripture that says "...God formed my inward parts and knit me together in my mother's womb..." is wrong? [12] No, because the bible is not speaking about the DNA process God has established to make a baby's body out of atoms and molecules. The DNA code and chemical reactions don't produce you (i.e., they don't create a person).

Look at what the Scripture does say; i.e., He procured (gathered) the substance a spirit is made of and He "erected my mind". This is when He built the part of your spirit that thinks and communicates. This is the moment you came into existence; this is the instant you became a life created in His image. At that moment, where nothing existed before, suddenly you could make the remarkable declaration "I am."

We realize the words "knit me together" can't be talking about your body made of atoms and molecules because it says "He knit *me* together in the womb", and you are not your body, you are spirit.

As we said in Chapter 2, the "real YOU" is not the earthly body, but is a spirit. The knitting in the womb, therefore, is God doing what only God can do, attaching a person, a spirit, to the human dust-body so the spirit can use the body's senses to experience the natural world. This is fantastic and described in the Bible like this:

[12] Note: always trust Scripture to be correct; it is always our understanding that is in error.

14 I will praise You; for I am fearfully and wonderfully made: marvelous are your works; and that my soul knows for sure.
Psalm 139:14

1 The burden of the word of the Lord for Israel, says the Lord, which stretched forth the heavens, and laid the foundation of the Earth, <u>and formed the spirit of man within him</u>.
Zechariah 12:1

You are fearfully and wonderfully made, but not by DNA in the womb. All the DNA does is form the scaffolding (human body) that will help you live and grow on the Earth and thereby shape your spirit's knowledge and personality. God, who is a spirit, has woven your spirit into your Earth-suit. ***Creating a spirit is something DNA could never do.***

Can you look beyond the illusion now? Can you see the truth? God made Creation so He could make lots of people, billions and billions of them, and His people are spirit in nature. When you look at other humans, you are looking at other spirits looking back at you through their bodies made of nothing but dust (atoms). Each of the spirits inside each of these bodies is a child of the living God, Creator of the universe.

So remember the truth about the first great illusion - you are not a physical body; you are a spirit. This is good news because it means there is a second great illusion you need to understand. We will discuss that in the next chapter.

God, who is a spirit, has woven your spirit into your human body. Creating a spirit is something DNA could never do.

4 The Second Great Illusion

Many people do not know what they really are. This lack of knowledge and the presence of incorrect beliefs can result in many problems throughout their lives. These include malformation of their soul, damage to their personality, and hurt caused to others. Always remember how deadly a wrong belief can be (remember the wagon train and the mirage in the desert).

In the last chapter, we read that we are fearfully and wonderfully made. "Fearfully" does not mean you are scary; it means when we look at how God made people and what they truly are, this makes goosebumps rise on our skin. What God is doing is so fantastic, so amazing, it leaves us in awe.

You are not just a person; you are a person in the form of a spirit created by God, and this fact has profound implications. Remember that your body, the thing you see when you look into a mirror, is not the real YOU. It is a complex, ongoing, chemical reaction made of dust, designed by God, that allows the real you to look into the world, our universe, and to have experiences with the things of our material world and with other spirits in a common environment. We are like His children in His nursery just beginning to learn all He wants us to know.

Through your physical body, a kind of scaffolding that your spirit permeated when it was "knitted in," you experience love; joy; sorrow; yearning; peace; poverty (or lack) and riches (or plenty); sickness and health; foods of all kinds; and of course all the plants, animals, and people of this world. While you are doing this, every other person in the world, using his or her own body, will be learning many of the same things you are learning, but in widely different circumstances, cultures, and ages (people have been doing this throughout history).

Most importantly, you will have relationships with others. You will learn to communicate, you will learn the difference between good and evil, and you will learn to love, and to forgive. All of these are critical to your functioning as a citizen of the Kingdom God has prepared for all His children.

Your body will someday grow old, wrinkly and eventually and die (perhaps smashed by a meteorite, run over by a truck, drowned in a tsunami, fatally damaged in a car crash, or by catching the Babylonian bungle fungus –who knows?). So what does this mean for you? For most people, who don't know they are spirit beings, death of the body is a scary idea. They don't like to think about it because they think it means the end of them. But now that you know the truth you must realize the idea of death just means the complex chemical reactions that allow the body to move, smell, see, hear, taste, and feel all stop working. *Death of your body can't hurt you because you are not your body.*

The body's death does nothing to you, except set you free from the human body you were knitted into. You see, **death is the second great illusion**. It is not what it looks like, and as far as your life goes, death on Earth is no more real than the mirage we discussed earlier. You will never stop existing. Why? Because God planned for His children to live with Him forever, long past the end of time.

When your body made from dust dies, your spirit separates from it and you go free. You take all you have learned and experienced with you.

Why is God doing all this? Because He wants a lot of people, billions of them to populate His Kingdom and to know Him and love Him forever. The experience each spirit obtains on Earth allows each person to have much in common with all the other people who will inhabit God's Kingdom, and yet be a different personality from every other person. These differences are very important in that they make each of God's children unique. Each person is shaped into a unique personality by their interaction with life on Earth.

> **PERSONALITY**: The set of emotional qualities, habitual ways of behaving (character), beliefs, moral strengths and weaknesses, knowledge, and assumed mannerisms, etc., that make one person different from another, and other attractive qualities (such as energy, friendliness, kindness, gentleness, cleanliness, facial expressions, posture, speech, tone of voice, and sense of humor) that make a person unique.

In summary: Think of what God is doing as something like this: He makes billions upon billions of new human spirits and lets them experience the natural world and to interact with other humans to create in each of them a unique personality. You may have seen how coins are struck, where a blank piece of metal is placed in a stamping machine which presses it hard against another piece of metal on which is carved the image of a man or historical building. The image is left pressed into the coin. God is forming personalities into His spirit children, but unlike the coins, which all come out exactly the same, every one of God's spirits returns to Him with different personalities because of different life experiences on Earth. And these are not just two-dimensional dents in the spirits like the dents pressed into a coin. These are records of whole lives lived in the four dimensions of space-time, full of experiences, memories, skills, and interactions with other human beings. What God is doing is truly amazing, and you are a part of this.

Why is God doing all this? Because He wants billions and billions of people to populate His Kingdom and to know Him and love Him forever.

5 When We are Free from our Earth-Suit

When we are free from our body, what will we find?

When your physical body goes back to the lifeless dust it was made from, what happens to you? Father God has anticipated this question. He has provided examples in the Bible about people coming back to life after dying. And even today He has allowed some people to go through the process of separating from their bodies, experiencing the continued-life, and then returning to their bodies. Why? We don't know for sure, but we can speculate that He allows this so they can tell the rest of us what they experienced. Hearing these testimonials increases our faith and hope, and in some cases helps a person (spirit) by giving them another chance. Our Creator is a God of love, forgiveness, and second chances.

Your body was grown in your mother's womb, and while that was happening God stitched the spirit-you into it. Then you underwent what is called the "first birth" where you were "born of water." "Born of water" describes your birth from your mother's womb where your baby-body floated in water (amniotic fluid). After birth you live your life learning all you can through your physical body in the natural world. Then when your body can no longer function, your spirit is set free.

> **Ok, so my body dies and I am set free. What is life like in that continued-life place?**

When you came into the world of planet Earth, you found all kinds of interesting things to do, and learn. Your liberation at the time of your body's death will release you into a whole new realm. You will find yourself in a place which is very different from planet Earth. You will be in God's territory, a place you cannot begin to imagine. We will call life after death "continued-life."

Let's see what the Bible says about this mysterious "continued-life" place. There is a passage of Scripture that recounts a conversation between Jesus and His disciples that revealed something about the place where spirits live.

> **14 And Jesus was casting out a devil, and it was a spirit that caused the man to be dumb (unable to speak). And it came to pass, when the devil was gone out, the dumb man began speaking. The folks watching this were amazed, and they wondered about Jesus.**
>
> **Luke 11:14**

Jesus was then accused of having an evil spirit inside Him that cast out the devil. He refuted this accusation by saying:

> **21 When an armed strong-man lives in his home, all that he owns is safe:**
> **22 But when a stronger man comes, and overpowers him, the stronger man takes from the weaker man all his protection, which the weaker man had trusted in, and the strong man gets control of all that the weaker man owned.**
> **23 He that is not with me is against me: and he that does not gather with me is scattering, not gathering.**
> **24 When the unclean spirit is gone out of a man, he walks through dry places, seeking rest; and finding none, he says, I will return into my house (the body of the man it left).**
> **25 And when it returns to the man, the evil spirit finds the man's body all cleaned up.**
> **26 So it goes and gets seven other spirits more wicked than him; and they enter in the man, and dwell in him, and the final condition of that man is worse off than before.**
>
> **Luke 11:21-24**

This passage reveals several things about the continued-life place. These are:

1. Along with God and His children (you), there are also unclean or evil spirits inhabiting the continued-life place.

2. It is possible for unclean spirits to enter a human body, somehow attach themselves to it, and live though it at the same time the person's spirit inhabits the body. They may be strong enough to take over some of the body's functions, such as speech. In fact, in a moment we will see that many spirits can occupy a body simultaneously. We will also see that this is not a very nice experience for a person.

3. Jesus is like the strong man. He has power and authority and is able to drive unclean spirits out of humans.

4. Spirits who are sent out of a human body do not like where they find themselves. Apparently it is like being in a dry desert, a wasteland, a lifeless place, and they are restless to find somewhere better. We can speculate that they prefer places where things are interesting to them, and where they can have power over people and things in our world. They seek rest (another person to infest). After being sent out they will try to return to the person they were sent out of, and will try to reenter.

5. There are spirits you would not want to associate with. Jesus called them unclean and evil.

Let's look at a passage of Scripture that describes the encounter between Jesus of Nazareth and a man whose human body was infested with evil spirits.

1 And they came over unto the other side of the sea, into the country of the Gadarenes.
2 And when Jesus was come off the ship, immediately a man with an unclean spirit came out of the tombs and met Him,
3 The man had his dwelling among the tombs; and no man could bind him, no, not with chains:
4 he had been often bound with fetters and chains, and

the chains had been tossed aside by him, and the fetters broken in pieces: and no man could control him.
5 Night and day, he was in the mountains, and in the tombs, crying, and cutting himself with stones.
6 But when he saw Jesus from some distance off, he ran and worshipped Him,
7 And cried with a loud voice, and said, What have I to do with you, Jesus, Son of the most high God? I implore you by God, that you not torment me.
8 He said this because Jesus said to the unclean spirit, Come out of the man.
9 And Jesus asked the spirit, what is your name? And the unclean spirit answered, saying, my name is Legion: for we are many.
10 And the spirit strongly begged Jesus that he would not be sent into the empty expanse.
11 Now there was on the mountains a great herd of swine feeding.
12 And all the devils begged Jesus, saying; Send us into the swine, that we may enter into them.
13 And Jesus immediately gave them permission. And the unclean spirits went out, and entered into the swine: and the herd ran violently down a steep place and into the sea, (they were about two thousand) and were drowned in the sea.
14 And they that fed the swine fled, and in the city and in the country they told what happened. And many went out to see what had happened.
15 And they came to Jesus, and saw the man that was possessed with the legion of devils, was now sitting, and clothed, and in his right mind: and they were afraid. Mark 5:1-15

There are several items of interest to us in this passage.

1. The man recognizes Jesus, which is puzzling because as far as we know he had never seen Jesus before. The spirit, speaking through

the man's vocal cords, addresses Jesus as "...son of the most high God." This is amazing since Jesus had trouble communicating this fact to His own disciples, and yet the spirits in this possessed man identified Jesus immediately. The explanation may be that the evil spirits in the man could see Jesus coming in the continued-life place and in the natural world at the same time.[13] It was clear to them who He was and how powerful He is.

2. It is important that the evil spirits recognized the power of Jesus and that they can see Him in the continued-life place. There is something about Him that is unmistakable, and the evil spirits knew immediately that He could force them out of the man they were infesting. Jesus has authority over these things. Remember what He said about the "strong man" in the previous verses.

3. The evil spirits beg Jesus to be sent to a specific place -- pigs. They apparently prefer to be sent into pigs instead of into the "empty expanse" or the "desolate place".

4. The evil spirits were talking via the man's vocal cords. This shows they were stronger than the man's spirit whom God had knitted into his human body. They had crowded him out of the use of his own body, which, because it was being controlled by many evil spirits, wandered and floundered around a graveyard, screaming, cutting itself, and causing the man to be unable to get along with any of the local people. The local folk had tried to chain him, but he had broken free and was now dragging his chains as he wandered the grave yard.

5. In this passage we again see the aversion evil spirits have to being cast out to where they will find nothing and remain restless and uncomfortable. In this case they call it "the countryside," "a distant land," "out of the country," or "out of the region," depending on what version of the Bible you have. In the Hebrew, it is called the "empty expanse" or the "space lying between two places or limits."

---

[13] Under certain circumstances humans can also see in this realm. See "In the Face of Evil – A Wakeup Call for Christians" by Roger Boehm. Specifically chapter 4 "The Quilt", see page 38, footnote 4.

They beg to be sent into nearby pigs, probably because they believed that at least in the pigs they could continue to experience the physical world through the pigs' senses. We can speculate they thought that since there were many pigs each one of their evil-spirit buddies would get a pig-body to rule.

6. It is likely the presence of the evil spirits so scared the pigs that they went into a blind, panicky charge into the sea and drowned.[14] At that point, the evil spirits probably disconnected from the pig-bodies and found themselves in that "empty expanse" they dislike.

There are other Scriptures where it is evident that evil spirits recognized Jesus.

> **40 Now when the sun was setting, all they that had any sick with various diseases brought them to him; and he laid his hands on every one of them, and healed them.**
> **41 And devils also came out of many of these sick people, crying out, and saying, You are the Christ the Son of God.**
> **And he rebuked them, not permitting them to speak: for they knew that he was Christ.[15]**
> **Luke 4:40-41**

Note that the spirits somehow know who Jesus is. Also note that the symptoms of sickness sometimes went away when "... devils... came out". This is a clue to us that all sickness is not due to biological pathogens.

---

[14] Pigs,, as we know them, can swim, which suggests that the poor pigs were not in control of their own bodies, and that the evil spirits who tried to inhabit them had not mastered control of a pig-body. They apparently could not coordinate the pigs' legs to produce a swimming motion.

[15] And why would Jesus not want the truth of who He really is revealed? A likely answer is that Jesus had come with a specific purpose in mind, and to be recognized and lifted up by the people as a powerful earthly king was not that purpose.

Here is another example.

> **33 And in the synagogue there was a man, which had a spirit of an unclean devil, and cried out with a loud voice,**
> **34 Saying, Let us alone; what have we to do with you, Jesus of Nazareth? Have you come to destroy us? I know who you are; the Holy One of God.**
> **35 And Jesus rebuked him, saying, keep quiet, and come out of him. And when the devil had thrown the man in their midst, he came out of him, and hurt him not. Luke 4:33-35**

In this example, the evil spirit (unclean devil) not only could see who Jesus really was, but seemed to have some foreknowledge that it would be Jesus who would eventually destroy all evil spirits.

When our physical bodies die are we going to just drift off into an empty expanse that spirits don't like to live in and which contains "evil" or "unclean" spirits? To answer this question, consider the following verses. This is Jesus speaking about what will happen after He dies:[16]

> **1 You don't need to worry; you believe in God, so also believe in me.**
> **2 In my Father's heaven are many mansions; if it were not so, I would have told you. I go to prepare a place for you.**
> **3 And if I go and prepare a place for you, I will come again, and receive you unto myself; that where I am, there ye may be also. John 14:1-3**

These words make it clear that you are valuable to God. Jesus was speaking just before He was to be killed on the cross. He was letting His followers know that He was leaving the natural world and that one of the

---

[16] Consider this thought: a man who speaks this way cannot be just a prophet or a wise holy-man, for no mere human being could possibly do these things. Jesus, therefore, must either be a deluded, crazy man or God Himself. Every one of us must decide which of these He is.

things He would do is to prepare a place for all His people. Last of all, He clearly says He will come again and receive those (believing in Him)[17] who are transitioning to the continued-life, so they won't be set adrift in a wasteland full of wandering evil spirits, but will be with Him (in Heaven). Do not worry about this. God is in control and He loves you.

Actually, with Jesus the continued-life place is more wonderful than you can imagine. Listen to Paul's writings to the church in Corinth about the death of our Earth-suit and what happens to our spirit.

> 1 **For we know that if our earthly house of this tabernacle were dissolved, we have a building of God, a house not made with hands, eternal in the heavens.**
> 2 **For in this we groan, earnestly desiring to be clothed upon with our house which is from heaven:**
> 3 **If so be that being clothed we shall not be found naked.**
> 4 **For we that are in this tabernacle do groan, being burdened: not for that we would be unclothed, but clothed upon, that mortality might be swallowed up of life.**
> 5 **Now he that hath wrought us for the selfsame thing is God, who also hath given unto us the earnest of the Spirit. 2 Cor 5;1-5**

You probably got the sense of that passage, but read it again with some of the old words, which were translated from Greek into English in the 1600s, fleshed out with the richness contained in the original Greek language set in italics.

> 1 **For we know that if our earthly *body, a temporary tent,* were dissolved, we have a *structure built by* God, *a habitable dwelling* not made with hands, *without end, never to cease, everlasting* in the**

[17] John 14:3 says nothing about believing in Him. The reason the author added and bracketed "believing in Him" is that in this passage He was speaking to believers. Biblical text makes it very clear that belief is fundamental to a person being able to be received by Jesus. This will be shown and explained in later chapters.

heavens.
2 *We groan for this*, earnestly desiring *to have put on over us our new habitation* which is from heaven:
3 So be that being *in our new dwelling* we shall not be found *without a body.*
4 For we that are in this *temporary tent* do groan, being *weighed down, but not with concern for losing our body*, but *to have put on over us our new habitation*, that *our body's ability to die* might be *replaced by life, real and genuine, active and vigorous, and devoted to God.*
5 Now He that has *worked this out for* us is God, Who also has given unto us the *Holy Spirit as a down payment and proof of what He will do.*

There you have it; Jesus has prepared a new body in Heaven for every righteous person. Life beyond the death of your body *is real*, and as you will learn, it is more real than the world you live in now.

One final thought on this subject. A group of Sadducees (Luke 20: 27) came to Jesus and asked a question to confirm their belief that there is no life after death. It was the custom of that day that when a man died his brother was expected to marry the widow to provide for her and her children. They proposed to Jesus that a man with seven brothers died. One of his brothers married his widow, and then he died. Another brother married her, and then he too died. This continued until all seven brothers had married her and died, and then she too died. The Sadducees question was "In the continued-life (the resurrection), whose wife will she be?"

34 And Jesus answering said unto them, the children of this world marry, and are given in marriage:
35 But they which shall be accounted worthy to get to heaven and be resurrected from the dead, neither marry, nor are given in marriage:
36 Neither can they die any more: for they are equal unto the angels; and are the children of God, being the children of the resurrection. Luke 20: 34-36

His answer tells us that Heaven will be fundamentally different from Earth. There will be no marriage, your nature will be like that of the Angels, and most wonderfully, you will be alive in a new body of an advanced design and will never die again.

The Sadducees were wrong! There is life after death.

Important Note to the Reader

Sometimes people have very difficult lives full of hurt and pain, death, broken relationships, and sorrow. This may seem overwhelming and a troubled human spirit may be tempted to use suicide to try to escape to the continued-life. Don't do it. God has a plan for each of our lives and escaping into what you think will be a new, wonderful life may cause harm to others you do not anticipate. There is also a chance your spirit is not ready to survive in that next world (more about this later).

Suicide is not a good option. Why? Because it does not fix any of the things wrong with you or your life. You will take what you are now to that new place. Troubles you now have can be fixed here on Earth.

And never forget the 6th of the Ten Commandments says we are not to commit murder. Suicide is the murder of self.

A better option is to "tough it out", talk to others about your difficulties, get help from a trusted counselor, pastor, teacher, or other adult. Learn, grow, heal and help others with what you learn. Focus on helping others and less on yourself. Let your Creator decide when it is time for you to come to Him. Don't take that choice away from Him.

Watch the testimonies in chapter 14 of some of the folks who tried suicide; Angie Fenimore and Tamara Laroux. Stay alive! Finish reading this book and you will find hope and joy. A wonderful future awaits you.

5. When we are Free from Our Earth-Suit

Our bodies, like this tree, undergo wear and tear, twisting and damage, and even the loss of parts as we age. Yet we are more than our bodies. The spirit that dwells within is cultured by the Creator for His purposes, and ultimately we will be perfected to please Him. Trust Him. Learn to know Him, and you will love Him as billions of other people do.

6 Who is this Jesus?

For you to have any chance of understanding your future, it's necessary to take a chapter to talk about the person Jesus. He is a real man in history, but a very unusual man. You have probably heard of Him, but chances are you have not met Him yet.

There have been many leaders, philosophers, gurus, military men, holy men, sages, high rulers, Califs, political leaders, and others who have risen in earthly power for a time and then gone to their grave. They have all been swallowed up by death over the centuries of human life on Earth. Some of these even claimed to be a god, demanding those under their power worship them. They too ended up going to their grave, dust back to dust. There is only one human being in all of history who was born, claimed to be the Creator, suffered death, conquered the grave, and returned to life. That's what sets Jesus apart from all other great leaders. After His death, he returned and revealed Himself to hundreds of individuals and continues to do so today. You don't need to doubt. Jesus will also reveal Himself to you. There are conditions, however, as disclosed in the Scripture below. These are the words of Jesus of Nazareth, known as the Christ.

> 21 **He that has my commandments, and obeys them, is one who loves me: and he that loves me shall be loved of my Father, and I will love him, *and will reveal myself to him.*** **John 14:21**

And there you have both a promise (I will reveal myself) and two conditions (having His commandments and obeying them.) This is one of the unique aspects of the Christian religion; it is the only religion whose Deity promises to reveal Himself to men and women. You never have to ask the question "Which religion is the true religion?" You never have to doubt again. Make meeting Him your quest, and your desire to meet Him will be satisfied. A personality who does not know Jesus is incomplete. Our spirit was designed to know Him and be in communion with Him.

He is interested in you seeking Him.

9a For the eyes of the LORD run to and fro throughout the whole earth, to show himself strong in the behalf of *them* whose heart *is* friendly[18] toward him. 2nd Chronicles 16:9a

God came into the natural world in a body (Jesus) made of Earth-dust just like yours. This makes him the Son of Man (born from a woman) and the Son of God (God the Father supernaturally provide the male part of the DNA to accomplish the conception.) This man Jesus was unique in many ways. He demonstrated the power to drive evil spirits out of people, to cure diseases, to control the weather, and to instantaneously cure physical deformities. But the most surprising thing Jesus demonstrated was that He could forgive sin.[19]

Since sin is committed against God, only God can forgive sin. Thus Jesus claimed to be God in the flesh, the Son of God, sent into the world for the forgiveness of sin. Now you might want to just blow this off and say that for Him to claim to be God is outrageous. The problem with this position is that Jesus demonstrated the ability to forgive sin, which pretty well proved He is who He claims to be. Here is how that happened:

2 They brought to Him a man sick of the palsy, lying on a bed: and when Jesus saw their faith he said to the sick man; Son, be of good cheer; your sins are forgiven.

Matthew 9:2

Palsy is an old word for *paralysis*, especially that which is accompanied by involuntary tremors. Those in the crowd were expecting Jesus to heal the man of his very visible, physical problem and instead were surprised that Jesus told him his sins were forgiven.

---

18 "Perfect" as used here from the Hebrew means "friendly" or "at peace with". You do not have to be faultless for God to love you and seek you.

19 Sin is the inherent tendency to do an act of transgression against divine law.. We all sin, that is to say we all miss the mark of living perfect lives, where the Creator defines what is perfect. Evaluate yourself; have you lived a sinless life?

3 And, behold, certain of the scribes said among themselves, "this man blasphemes."
Matthew 9:3

Blaspheme means to treat God or sacred things disrespectfully. These words of Jesus were blasphemous in the scribes' religious viewpoint because everyone knew that only God Himself could forgive sins. So any man making this claim was arrogant and outrageous in the minds of the scribes. What they heard was Jesus saying "I am God."

4 And Jesus knowing their thoughts said "Why do you think evil in your hearts?
5 Is it easier to say Thy sins are forgiven; or to say, Arise, and walk? Matthew 9:4-5

Jesus knew what they're thinking. He also knew it's impossible to see a man's sins being forgiven. So to prove the sins were forgiven He pointed out that only God can heal the man's paralysis. Only god can make him walk again. Jesus, who called Himself the "Son of Man", then said:

6 But so that you may know that the Son of man has power on Earth to forgive sins, (then he said to the man with the palsy) Arise, take up thy bed, and go to your house.
7 And the man got up, and departed to his house.
8 But when the multitudes saw it, they marveled, and glorified God, who had given such power unto men.
Matthew 9:6-8

Thus Jesus demonstrated something only God can do: the instant healing of the man's paralysis, and by inference, the forgiveness of sins.

But Jesus did more than this. He came back to life after dying on the cross. He did this to prove to us who He is and to demonstrate for us the death of our human body is not the end of life. Paul the apostle says it this way:

1 I declare unto you the gospel (Good News) which I preached to you, which you have received, and now

believe;
2 This belief allows you to be saved, if you remember what I preached to you, unless you have believed unsuccessfully.
3 For I gave you what I learned, that Christ died for our sins according to the Scriptures;
4 And that he was buried, and that he rose again (came back to life) the third day after his burial, and this is according to and in agreement with the Scriptures;
5 And after Jesus' death he was seen by Cephas, then by one of Jesus' twelve disciples;
6 After that, he was seen by more than five hundred brethren at once; most of whom are still living (at the time this was written), though some have died by now.
7 After that, he was seen by James; then of all the apostles.
8 And last of all I saw Him too, like a baby being born late. **1 Corinthians 15:1-8**

A personality who does not know Jesus is incomplete. Our spirits were designed to know Him and be in communion with Him. He is interested in you seeking Him.

Everyone should consider this man Jesus and decide what to believe about Him. Was He just a man? Was He more than just a man? Consider the following verses: Philip asked Jesus to show God to him.

Jesus said to him, have I been with you so long, and yet you haven't known who I am, Philip? A person that sees me has seen the Father; so why do you say, Show us the Father?

John 14:9

He met a woman at a well and confirmed that He is the Messiah that all mankind had been waiting for.

> **The woman said to Him, "I know that Messiah is coming; and when He comes He will tell us everything."**
> **Jesus said to her, "I who speak to you, I am the Messiah."** **John 4:25-26**

And here are other Scriptures pertaining to the Deity of Christ:

Jesus did not start at His birth in Bethlehem.

> **He existed in the beginning with God.**
> **John 1:2**

Jesus will exist forever.

> **But to the Son He says: "Your throne, O God, is forever and ever;"** **Hebrews 1:8**

Jesus and Father God are not two gods.

> Jesus said: **"I and the Father are one."**
> **John 10:30**

Moses asked God for His name. This is God's answer.

> **And God said to Moses, "I AM WHO I AM"; and He said, "Thus you shall say to the sons of Israel, "I AM has sent me to you."**
> **Exodus 3:14**

In the last Scripture cited above, God called Himself "I Am". God is saying that more important than His name is the fact that *He really exists.* Because God is spirit and cannot be seen, this is the fundamental issue mankind has struggled with through the centuries. Is God real? In the New Testament after God has come in the flesh we see:

58 Jesus said to them, "Truly, truly, I say to you, before Abraham was born, I am." John 8:58

Here Jesus makes a statement only God could make. Basically He says, "Before Abraham was born, I existed." This could only be true of God. He also is also reminding them of what He told Moses.

The above Scriptures have been pulled out of context. You are invited to go to each and read the text that accompanies each one. If you will do that, you will see that according to the Bible, Jesus is God, Savior, and Creator of the universe, who came in the flesh of a human body. God knit His own Spirit into the dust-body of Jesus of Nazareth, just as you are a spirit in your own human body. And now you know what Christian people mean when they say "God has come in the flesh and dwelt among us".

To love us more, He experienced the very same life on Earth we all live through, including all its troubles and pains, including His own death. He knows us well and loves us very much.

You need to be ready for that day when your Earth-suit quits working, so consider the following: You know that when your body dies your spirit is set free. You may find yourself in a place not like Earth, a place that is "dry" (lifeless), and an empty expanse that you may find uncomfortable. Not only that, but there will be other spirits hanging out there, some of whom are "evil" or "unclean." These evil spirits apparently are like a bunch of orphaned, malevolent children, or even like parasites in the spiritual world. They seek to attach to a human body, a portal that connects them into the space-time universe God created for man.

Before we go further, we need to mention where these evil, unclean things came from, and why they exist at all. The answer involves a Heavenly spiritual war and the fall of a created being named Satan (Lucifer).

12 How did you fall from heaven, O Lucifer, son of the morning! How is it that you who did weaken entire nations, are cut down to the ground!
13 It is because you have said in your heart, I will ascend into heaven, I will exalt my throne above the stars of God: I will sit also upon the mount of the

congregation, in the sides of the north:
14 I will ascend above the heights of the clouds; I will be like the most High (God). Isaiah 14:12-14

7 And there was war in heaven: Michael and his angels fought against the dragon; and the dragon fought along with his angels,
8 But he lost the battle; and he and his angels were removed from heaven.
9 Then Satan was cast out of heaven, and Satan, which deceives the whole world, was cast out into the Earth, and his angels were cast out with him.
Revelation 12:7-9

18 Jesus said unto them, I saw Satan fall from heaven as fast as a flash of lightning. Luke 10:18

People call this evil-spirit leader *Satan* or the *Devil*, and his evil-spirit followers are called *devils* or *demons*. If you have trouble accepting the idea of evil spirits, devils and demons you're invited to read Appendix D for more information and some interesting thoughts.

7 The Perfect Personality

The exciting, miraculous truth we have been discussing is that life does not end at the death of your human body made of dust. Imagine that! Life is eternal. This means that perceiving your environment, going places, having adventures, meeting people, making new relationships, having a relationship with your Creator, and expressing yourself artistically and creatively can go on forever. Plus you will be able to meet people from all of human history. You will no longer be bound by time, which acts like a constant pressure on us to get things done. On top of this you will be able to see and communicate with your Creator, the most loving father you can imagine. So save up your questions.

The One who created the universe, and created us, said in the Bible that we were created in His image. God has a personality, and that's why ours is so important. Here is a partial list of some of the attributes of God found in the Bible. These are all found in Jesus, who was God in the flesh on Earth. Remember that we are to be like Him.

HOLY – pure, without stain or blemish in our thoughts and actions.

JUST – in decisions and actions towards others; fair, impartial, objective, unbiased, unprejudiced, evenhanded, appropriate, proper, fitting, correct, moral, ethical and good.

GOOD – never doing evil things, being upright, virtuous, wholesome and blameless; having no part in ungodliness.

MERCIFUL – willing to forgo punishments for wrongs done to Him or His way.

GRACIOUS – willing to give grace toward our sins, to remove the memory of them as far as the east is from the west.

LONGSUFFERING – patient, willing to wait for the benefit of another, slow to anger.

TRUTHFUL – never speaking untruth, trustworthy in everything.

TEMPERATE – measured, peaceable, composed - having strong self-control.

FORGIVING – not clinging to wrongs done in the past by others.

WISE – prudent, sensible, judicious, clever, learned - able to make good decisions using the information one has.

LOVING – the basic nature of caring for others, particularly agape love, the type of love that asks for nothing in return.

GENTLE – having a mild temperament or behavior, being kind or tender, being moderate in action, effect or degree. Peaceful. Joyful.

STEADFAST – not wishy-washy, having a constant, trustworthy character.

ABLE TO BE RIGHTEOUSLY ANGRY – made angry by right reasons such as wickedness, evil deeds, evil plotting, hatred, and unforgiveness.

MEEK – possessing enormous power under immense self-control.

FAITHFUL – you can count on Him to be Himself, trustworthy, a promise keeper, and with your best interests in mind.

RIGHTEOUS – having no sin. Never missing the mark. Holy, pure and Blameless.

We are all called to be like God. However, you can tell by reading the list above that none of us humans have personalities that express all these godly characteristics. In fact, some of us are really nasty people, even evil. There are people who enslave, steal, murder, hate, lie, and bully others and don't give a second thought about it. There are people who drink too much and destroy their families by their actions. There are people who will kill God's little people in their mothers' wombs for in exchange for money. There are people who use illegal substances that damage the body that God has given them. There are people who hate for all kinds of reasons and some refuse to forgive other who have hurt them. Some act worse than others, but all of us have personalities that deviate from God's perfect nature. These are all examples of deviation from righteous, God-like living. This deviation we call "sin." All of us have sin in us. Sin causes us to miss the mark of God's perfect holiness.

You can think of this sin in us as an inherent tendency to do immoral, evil, or wicked acts; commit wrongdoings; transgress against God's law; or commit crimes, offenses, misdeeds, iniquity, and vice. Sin is also involved in wrong actions that do not look as serious as murder. For example, if a young person's mother asks the child to clean up his or her room or to do some other work and the child refuses to do it, he or she has sinned by breaking one of the Ten Commandments – You Shall Honor Your Mother and Father. When the child does that, they have willfully stuck their thumb into God's eye, and broken one of the ten laws He gave us to follow. Basically they are, in their own small way, in rebellion against the Creator of the universe.

Do you see the difficulty God is in? He's placing spirits in Earth-bodies so they can grow and develop personalities so they can live with Him in Heaven forever. But this won't work because God is holy and pure. He cannot and will not coexist with sin.

If you wonder why He can't coexist with sin, consider these two examples:

Example 1: Suppose you're thirsty and someone placed two glasses of water on the table in front of you and told you that you could only pick one of them to drink. Both glasses contain the same amount of water. But then you are told that one glass was filled with clean water (this water is clear) and the other glass was filled from a toilet bowl at the local gas station restroom (this water is cloudy). Which one would you want to drink?

Most people would be revolted at the thought of drinking the toilet bowl water, even if it appeared clear. The reason for their objection to the toilet water is the same reason our Father God cannot tolerate sin in His Heaven. The toilet water is contaminated with things dangerous to humans like viruses and bacteria associated with excrement. Drinking it would cause illness throughout your entire body and may even kill you. Likewise, a sinful soul is contaminated with impurity, injustice, wickedness, a lack of mercy, ungratefulness, impatience, falsehood, unforgiveness, anger, and unfaithfulness, among other negative personality characteristics. To have these characteristics in Heaven, all of which are opposite God's nature, would turn Heaven into a kind of Hell.

You might argue that a just little sin shouldn't be a problem. If this is your view, then consider what would happen if you took the glass of clean water, dumped much of it out, and then filled it back up using water from the toilet. Now you have just a little fecal matter in your water (just a little sin in your liquid Heaven). Would you drink from the glass which is half toilet water? The answer again is no, because it could still make you sick. Likewise, Father God in His wisdom will only allow completely righteous souls in His Heaven. (Do not fear. He has provided a way for you to be with him. Read on.)

A sinful soul is a nasty thing, rotten, full of corruption and vile factors.

Example 2: The Bible uses the idea of smells to help us understand how Father God perceives righteousness. It says that Jesus is the only righteous man, and 2 Corinthians 2:15 says that (when we have invited Jesus into our hearts) our lives are Christ-like, a pleasing fragrance to God. For God righteousness is pleasing to be around and to associate with just like the smell of a pleasing aftershave lotion or perfume.

One summer, the author took a long trip away from home, but when he departed he forgot to take out the kitchen trash, which happened to contain the remains of a chicken dinner. While he was gone and the apartment was closed up with the air conditioning turned off these scraps decayed and molded. This caused the horrible smell of rotting chicken to fill the whole apartment. He returned home, and when the front door was opened he instantly knew what he had done because the apartment reeked. His little "Heaven" was badly contaminated to the point he could not stand to be inside. He had to hold his nose, close up the kitchen trash bag, and take it to the dumpster. He then had to open many windows and let the apartment air out before the smell of that living space was tolerable.

If righteousness smells good to God, then unrighteousness could be compared to the stench of rotting chicken. God would not want to be near it or even in the same room with it. A sinful soul is a nasty thing: rotten, full of corruption and vile factors. Other souls He has created and who live in Heaven could not live with unrighteousness either. Phew! And neither could you.

So how does God handle it when billions of His new spirit-persons are contaminated with sin during their life on Earth? Let's see what the Bible says. This is described in a parable (story) told by Jesus – the Bible calls it the parable of the Rich man and Lazarus.

19 There was a certain rich man, who was clothed in purple and fine linen, and who ate wonderful meals every day:
20 And there was a certain beggar named Lazarus, who lay at the rich man's gate, full of sores,
21 desiring to be fed with the crumbs which fell from the rich man's table: moreover the dogs came and licked his sores.
22 And it came to pass, that the beggar died, and was carried by the angels into Abraham's bosom (heaven), and the rich man also died, and was buried;
23 And in hell the rich man lifted up his eyes, while being tormented, and saw Abraham and Lazarus in heaven far away.
24 And he cried out and said, "Abraham, have mercy on me, and send Lazarus, that he may dip the tip of his finger in water, and cool my tongue; for I am tormented in this flame."
25 But Abraham said, "Son, remember that you during your life received good things, while Lazarus received evil things: but now he is comforted, and you are tormented.
26 And beside all this, between us and you there is a great gulf fixed: so that anyone who wanted to come over to you cannot; neither can you come over to us."
27 Then the rich man said, "I pray, father Abraham

that you would send Lazarus to my father's house:
28 For I have five brothers; so that Lazarus may warn them of this place, otherwise they also will come into this place of torment."
29 Abraham said, "They have Moses and the prophets; let them hear them."
30 And he said, "No, father Abraham that is not enough. But if someone went to them from the dead, they will believe him and repent."
31 And Abraham said unto him, "If they won't listen to Moses and the prophets, neither will they be persuaded, even if somebody comes back from the dead.[20] Luke 16:19-31

According to this passage not all personalities are welcome in God's Heaven. The rich man was not allowed in Heaven because he ignored the needs of the beggar. Some of the characteristics of the rich man's personality may have included lack of compassion (caring for others), greed, selfishness, and perhaps a belief in his superiority over the dirty beggar lying at his gate. Humility and kindness were missing. He failed to obey God's laws on Earth (we are commanded to love our neighbors as ourselves). He was not a righteous man.

Here are some key ideas we can learn from this story:

1. After your body dies and the real YOU is set free, God sends angels to fetch you. (Verse 22)

2. The angels greet the spirits recently separated from their bodies. Some are taken to a wonderful place, called Heaven (called Abraham's bosom in this story), which God has prepared for His children, and the others go to a terrible place call Hades (or Hell). (Verse 22)

3. Spirits in Hell can see those in Heaven, but there is a

[20] Astute readers will catch Jesus' tongue-in-cheek reference in verse 31 to His own death and resurrection. He was predicting that those who would not listen to Moses and the Prophets would also not be persuaded by the Savior's death and return from the grave.

> great chasm between these two places that no soul can cross over. (Verse 23-24)

So God handles sin in His created beings by separating them into one of two places.

God in His wisdom and love has provided a way for all of us to come to Heaven, no matter what we have done. Read on…

The Second Death

A person still alive on Earth and corrupted by sin is called "lost." These are persons who have failed in their human bodies to be righteous enough to be one of those God is seeking for His Heaven. Going to Hell is called the second death.

But don't worry, God in His wisdom and love has provided a way for all of us to come to Heaven, no matter what we have done. There is a very important personality characteristic called "righteousness" that you gain when all your sins are washed away. When that happens, your righteousness will look as pure and as holy as the righteousness of Jesus: sinless. Righteousness is necessary for you to be pleasing to God (for your presence to be a sweet aroma to Him).

Here is another way to look at this whole picture. This is also from the Bible. To God, people who lack righteousness are like weeds in His people-garden on Earth. The Bible uses the word "tares" (a type of weed[21]) to describe sinful people, but describes the people who have righteousness as wheat, a good crop. Tares are weeds that are hard to distinguish from the good wheat.

A person grows within their human body until that person is ripe (when God judges that he or she is ready to separate from the body and be

[21] The tares mentioned in the Bible are thought to be a weed called darnel. This weed looks similar to wheat, but is often poisonous due to the presence of a fungus called ergot that grows on it. At harvest time wheat and tares are easy to separate because the tares stand tall while the fruit-laden heads of wheat bow over.

harvested by the angels). As Jesus puts it:

> **30 "At the time of the harvest I will say to the angels, gather up all the tares and bind them up to burn them (Hades), but gather the wheat into my barn (Heaven)." Matthew 13:30**

We said earlier that spirits live forever and they do not die after a period of time like the human body does; however, they can be destroyed. Jesus revealed this piece of knowledge when He was speaking about not having fear of evil men. Jesus said:

> **28 "Don't fear people who can kill your body, but are not able to kill the soul: but rather fear Him (God) who is able to destroy both soul and body in hell." Matthew 10:28**

In this Scripture the purpose of Hell is revealed. It is God's way of undoing the creation of a spirit that has become so corrupted by sin that it cannot be allowed into Heaven and cannot be redeemed. It cannot be allowed to continue to exist. It is like that rotten tomato growing in your garden, worth only to be plucked off and discarded into the mulch bin (tomato Hell) where heat and bacteria will turn it into mulch.

What then is this righteousness that God desires in all the spirit beings (people) He creates? Do you have it? If you think you might not have it, how can you get it? Are you one of the "lost" who does not have righteousness and is headed toward Hell?

Be assured that righteousness can be part of your personality. This will be discussed in the later chapters, but first we will look at the results of sin.

8 The Results of Sin

Sin is nasty. It is a killer. The first sin became evident when Adam and Eve disobeyed God by eating the fruit He had forbidden. The presence of sin in the human race, in every man, woman, and child is unmistakable. Just turn on the television and watch the news. You will see people acting and relating to others in very ungodly ways. These people would totally trash Heaven if they were allowed in.

The media is full of stories exposing sin in action: news of a father who killed his two preschool children, his wife, and then himself, news that someone put a bomb on a bus, news of a bank being robbed. Someone received too much change from the cashier, and knew it, but did not tell the cashier and did not return the money. Someone lusts after someone else's spouse.

Sin abounds. You don't have to look very far to see evidence of people missing the mark of God's perfect Holiness.

Be assured that not one person who sins will escape God's eye. He knows you very well, and you cannot hide from him what you do (or think). Yet God has not made pleasing Him difficult. He gave us the Ten Commandments to make it clear what He expects of us. He would be very happy if we kept all ten of His simple, reasonable rules while we lived on Earth. Examine your own life. Compare the Ten Commandments to the way you live. Have you missed the mark?

The Ten Commandments

1. You shall have no other gods before Me.

Do you honor God (the Father of us all) by obeying Him? Are there things in your life that you hold more important than what He wants? Do you lift up (place importance on) an amulet, magic spells, possessions, philosophies, or scientific theories rather than the invisible Creator of everything? Do you devote much of your lifetime to "things"? Do you devote so much time to a sport, a boat, money, drugs, video games, television, etc. that it is as if you are worshiping those things? Look at where you spend your money, and you will see what you worship. Do you ignore Him day in and day out? Do you worship some god invented by mankind?

2. You shall not make for yourself a carved image—any likeness of anything that is in Heaven above, or that is in the earth beneath, or that is in the water under the earth; you shall not bow down to them nor serve them.

Do you pray to or worship images or statues of people, birds, or beasts? Do you consider God as equal to any part of His creation? Do you worship trees, or cows, or monkeys, your ancestors, or believe that a god lives in trees, frogs, rivers, or other *created* things? Has your mind replaced the living God with the enormous mass of dead atoms, molecules, and empty space of the universe (all there is or ever will be)?

3. You shall not take the name of the LORD your God in vain, for the LORD will not hold *him* guiltless who takes His name in vain.

Have you ever cursed using God's name? Have you ever valued His name so little that you made Him and all He stands for cheap or worthless? Have you ever voted with those who removed prayer from our schools, or pushed to remove any remembrance of Him from our coins, holidays, and public places? Do you laugh and scoff at those who take God seriously? Are you more comfortable when the word "God" or the name "Jesus" is not mentioned? If so, you are taking Him (and all He stands for) in vain (as worth little).

4. Remember the Sabbath day, to keep it holy.

Do you keep the Sabbath day special in your mind? Do you remember Him that day by joining with others to do good works in His name or to worship Him in a community setting where possible?

5. Honor your father and your mother, that your days may be long upon the land which the LORD your God is giving you.

Do you honor your father and mother in the way you treat them and remember them? Do you speak kindly to them and about them to others? If you are still in their home, do you honor them by obeying them without hassle and argument? Do you dishonor them by living off them without putting in your fair share of work and money? Have you created children and then abandoned them to your parents for their care and upbringing?

6. You shall not murder.

Have you ever murdered someone - caused his or her body to stop functioning - out of your anger or desire for something they have that you wanted, or because of something they did to you? Jesus said if you hold hatred in your heart toward someone, then you have essentially committed murder. Have you considered suicide? It is the murder of self. It is wrong because it interrupts God's plans for your life. Don't do it. Trust Him.

7. You shall not commit adultery.

Jesus said if you even look upon another with lustful thoughts, you have committed adultery. Have you committed adultery?

8. You shall not steal.

Have you stolen anything? Have you stolen something by not taking an action you should have taken – such as not returning money the cashier gave you by mistake? Do you perform unauthorized copying of games, movies, or music? Do you cheat on your taxes? Have you stolen by misleading someone else about the truth to get money or other benefits from them? Have you worked a con to get money out of others?

9. You shall not bear false witness against your neighbor.

Have you lied, or stretched the truth when talking about someone else in order to get some advantage for you, or to hurt someone's reputation, or to get someone in trouble? Have you participated in "false news" to gain an advantage over an opponent or to deceive others? Have you applied "spin" to a story to skew the narrative to control or manipulate others or make you look good or get your way?

10. You shall not covet anything that is your neighbor's.

Have you ever desired wrongfully, inordinately, or without proper concern for the rights or needs of others?

If you have broken or failed to keep any of these commandments, you can be assured the spiritually deadly infection of sin is operating within you. You are lost. When your body dies, the harvesting angels will easily see the stain of that sin and will gather you as a tare, not as wheat. You will not be able to enter Heaven, and will have to go to where there are other spirits contaminated with sin and evil. Worse than that, you will be separated from God, ***which is horrible because being with God as His child is why you were created***. You were meant to be with Him, to enjoy Him and love Him forever, and be loved by Him. Instead you (your spirit) will have to be separated from God and destroyed in the fires of Hades.

The Bible speaks about this

20 "The soul that sins, it shall die."
Ezekiel 18:20

23 "The wages of sin is death."
Romans 6:23

These passages are not speaking of the first death, the death of your human body, but the second death, the destruction of a sin-infected soul in the fires of Hell.

The Scriptures say:

10 "There is none righteous, no, not one."
Romans 3:10

This is saying that no one on Earth can achieve righteousness by his or her own doing. There is only one chance for you. Read on!

Just as a new baby must have mature lungs to be ready to breathe and provide oxygen to its bloodstream the minute it is born, or it will die, there is a personality characteristic that must be part of you the instant you separate from your body at its death, or you will die the "second death."

9 Righteousness and Your Personality

Righteousness Is Very Important

There is something you need in your personality to help you survive in that place of continued-life. A new baby will die if it does not have mature lungs the minute it is separated from its umbilical cord at birth. Likewise, there is a personality characteristic that must be part of you the instant you separate from your human body. If you are not ready you will die the second death (destruction in Hades).

God holds the power to save lost people, and He has provided a way for you to obtain that personality characteristic..

Many New Testament Scriptures talk about salvation. Let's look at just a few to understand:

> 14 **And as Moses lifted up the serpent in the wilderness, even so must the Son of man be lifted up:**
> 15 **That whosoever believes in Him should not perish, but have eternal life.**
> 16 **For God so loved the world, that he gave his only begotten Son, that whosoever believes in Him should not perish, but have everlasting life.**
> 17 **For God didn't send his Son into the world to condemn the world; but that the world through Him might be saved.**
> 18 **He that believes on Him is not condemned: but he that believes not is condemned already, because he has not believed in the name of the only begotten Son of God.**
> 19 **And this is the condemnation, that light is come into the world, and men loved darkness rather than light, because their deeds were evil.**
> 20 **For every one that does evil hates the light, and does not come to the light, because if he did his deeds would be criticized.**

21 But he that does truth comes to the light so that his deeds may be made visible, and be revealed as godly works.

John 3:14-21

Consider these points:

1. John 3:14 says the Son of man (Jesus) must be "lifted up." This is referring to when Jesus was nailed to the cross while it was lying on the ground. As the cross was raised to a vertical position, Jesus was lifted up with it to hang there and die. His crucifixion also lifted Him up in the sense that it draws attention to His death and resurrection. Each of us can "lift Him up" by telling His story to others.

2. Verse 15 tells why He had to be lifted up: so that anyone who believed would not perish but have eternal life. The word *perish* is not referring to the human body dying, but rather the second death; being gathered by the angels for Hades and the destruction of your soul. So it is saying that ***anyone who believes in Jesus and His death on the cross for the forgiveness of sins will not be gathered as a tare but will be gathered as wheat.***

3. The well-known John 3:16 passage tells us why God has granted us everlasting life through His son. It is because of His great love for us.

4. Verse 17 says that by believing in what Jesus has done for us all, our spirits change status from "lost" to "saved," a change from tare to wheat, a change in destination from Hades to Heaven.

The act of believing what God has said about why Christ came and died imparts to us Jesus' righteousness. This is really good news!

Righteousness is the moral state of perfection required by God for someone to enter Heaven. It is having right standing with God as if you had never sinned.

It is up to us to purposefully make righteousness part of our personality. It is a choice, our choice. Righteousness through Jesus Christ is a free gift from God. However we must accept the free gift by choosing to believe that Jesus died for us and that this is sufficient to save us. This is the gospel of Jesus Christ.

Jesus said:

> **15 If ye love me, keep my commandments.**
> **16 And I will pray the Father, and he shall give you another Comforter, that he may abide with you forever;**
> **17 Even the Spirit of truth; whom the world cannot receive, because it sees Him not, neither does it know Him: but you know Him; for he dwells with you, and shall be in you.**
>
> **John 14:15-17**

This means when you receive the free gift of God's forgiveness through accepting Jesus, you have expressed a desire for God to dwell in you. He will then do that, as the Holy Spirit, and begin the work to free you from slavery to sin and give you help in doing what is right.

Some people worry about God's spirit coming to dwell within them. They think of those horror movies where someone is possessed by an evil spirit and they do all kinds of gross things. Like levitating over their bed, spinning their head round and round, and making horrible sounds. God's spirit is not at all like that. His is a pleasant presence that is not even noticeable much of the time. God's spirit, Holy Spirit, is kind, gentle, loving and willing to help you in many areas of your life. We were designed by Him to be in close fellowship with Him. Think of Holy Spirit as a kind father with your best interest at heart.

The following passage clearly says what it is like to have Holy Spirit dwell with you.

> **10 I will rejoice greatly in the LORD, My soul will exult in my God; For He has clothed me with garments of salvation, He has wrapped me with a robe of righteousness, As a bridegroom decks Himself with a garland, And as a bride adorns herself with her jewels.**
>
> **Isaiah 61:10**

When you believe what God has said about Jesus, and invite the Holy Spirit in, it will be as if He cloaks you in righteousness. You will be clean and free from all your sin.

One final comment…

> **14 Now after that John was put in prison, Jesus came into Galilee, preaching the gospel of the kingdom of God,**
> **15 And saying the time is fulfilled, and the kingdom of God is at hand: repent, and believe the gospel.**
>
> **Mark 1:14-15**

Notice the use of the word *repent* in verse 15. Repent means to turn from sin, agreeing with God that you have sinned, and dedicating yourself to living a sinless life to the best of your ability. Without repentance your belief is in question, for how can you truly believe Jesus went through that horrible death on the cross for you and then continue sinning with no effort on your part to stop? You cannot fool God. [22]

[22] Actually, repentance is not a one-time event. Once you believe and invite Holy Spirit to live in you, He gives you power to make good choices. But know that if you sin again, Satan will try to make you ashamed over that sin to try to separate you from Father God. Don't fall for that trick. Just go to God in prayer (you don't need a priest) and confess your sin (He knows everything we do anyway). You will be forgiven and will no longer be a slave to sin.

10 How can Jesus be the "Only" Way to Heaven?

Many people ask the question, "How can Jesus be the only way to obtain acceptance by God?" They believe there must be other ways to reach God and His Heaven. What they don't realize is that there really is only one way to pleasing God. Let's look at that.

Jesus spoke of Himself when He said the following:

> **13 "Enter through the narrow gate. For wide is the gate and broad is the road that leads to destruction, and many enter through it.**
> **14 But small is the gate and narrow the road that leads to life, and only a few find it.**
> **Matthew 7:13-14**

He also said:

> **9 I am the door: by me if any man enters in, he shall be saved, and shall go in and out, and find pasture.**
> **10 The thief cometh not, but for to steal, and to kill, and to destroy: I am come that they might have life, and that they might have it more abundantly.**
> **11 I am the good shepherd: the good shepherd gives his life for the sheep. John 10:9-11**

The gate is narrow because the bible says that believing that Jesus died as atonement[23] for our sins is the only way those sins can be removed.

No other person,
no other belief system,
no great religious leader
no politician,
no psychological counseling,

---

[23] Atonement – paying the penalty for sin in full, compensation, reparation. Also called propitiation.

no good deed you might do,
no gift of money,
no charitable service,
no dying in battle with an infidel,
no belonging to a particular church,
no relationship to any human being
can provide you with righteousness.

Jesus is the only way to obtain the righteousness you need. The wide gate is everything else in the world besides Jesus and His death on the cross for you.

Here's another way of looking at salvation through Jesus only. When God created Earth, He pre-established laws that govern the way the Earth (the natural world) operates. One of the laws is called the law of gravity. This law says if you step off a cliff you will fall. Gravity constantly pulls downward, and gravity is good because it keeps all the water, people, and animals from floating off into space. Life wouldn't be possible without gravity. But you can ignore the law of gravity and walk too close to the edge of a cliff and slip. As you are falling to your death, yelling...

"The law of gravity is unfair!"

...will not help you. The law of gravity acts on you whether you are prudent or stupid, and your human body made of electric and nuclear fields and empty space can be destroyed by the effects of the law of gravity.

Likewise, God has established that believing in His son Jesus as Savior is necessary for all your sins to be removed. This is good, because it makes coming to Heaven easy and it causes unrepentant, corrupt, sin-racked, souls to be automatically separated from Heaven. When your body dies, and your spirit is cast free into the continued-life place, the principle of forgiveness through the death of Jesus Christ immediately operates on you. If you believe what God said, the angels will see you as wheat (no sin). You will be taken to Heaven to be in fellowship with God and His people forever. That's a really good deal!

On the other hand, if you do not believe in Christ's sacrificial death on the cross is sufficient to remove your sins, then the moment you enter the continued-life place you have slipped off the cliff and are falling downward toward the pit of Hell. At that moment yelling...

"It's unfair that God requires me to believe in Jesus!"

...will not help you. God requiring you to believe in His son's sacrificial death acts on you whether you are prudent or stupid, and your sin-filled spirit can be destroyed in Hell by the effects of your failure to believe what your Creator has said.

God can't tolerate your sin in Heaven any more than you could drink the stinky, feces-laden toilet-bowl water. God is not mean or narrow-minded; He is giving you a free choice and offering you an easy pass, a free ticket. He has taken all of your sin and its consequences onto Himself on the cross when He was crucified if you will only repent[24] and believe what He says. But you must trust Him; you must believe Christ has done this for you.

People often complain that Christianity is narrow-minded because it claims that accepting Jesus' death on the cross for the forgiveness of our sins is the only way to please God. Seeing this claim of Christianity as narrow-minded is just a choice that some people make. **They could choose to see it as God making the way to Heaven as simple and easy as possible.** He has made it very clear how to please Him - just believe what He says! We take too lightly the depth of God's love. We just can't believe that we can be saved and loved by Him without doing some work for Him. We feel like we need to pay a penalty, not realizing that Jesus has already paid the penalty for us.

Your relationship with Jesus when your body dies will be your relationship when you are in your spirit form. If you believe that your sins are not forgiven, this will carry over into the continued-life *and you will not be covered by His righteousness.*

18 Verily I say unto you, Whatsoever ye shall bind on Earth shall be bound in heaven: and whatsoever ye

---

[24] Repent means to turn from sin, feeling regret for your sins, and dedicating yourself to living a sinless life to the best of your ability

shall loose on Earth shall be loosed in heaven.
Matt 18:18

Why would the Creator design us this way? Here is a way to look at this that makes sense. Remember the story in Matthew 14:30 where Peter was able to walk out on the water towards Jesus. He could stay with Christ on *top of the water* only while he had sufficient belief. The instant he took his eyes off of Christ, his faith faltered, he doubted, and he *began to sink* into the deep, dark sea. Your heavenly Father God does not want there to be a possibility after you reach the continued-life place that your belief in His forgiveness falters, breaking the fellowship He has with you. When your body dies, you step out into an enormous, vast, new sea. You must have faith in Jesus. If your mind is stuck in unbelief, you will sink unimpeded into the deep, dark pit. You will not even be able to raise your eyes back up to Jesus and call for His help to stop the sinking ***because forever more you will not believe what He has done for you.***

God has said the wheat and tares will be separated, and this is how it happens.

> He has made it very clear how to please Him: just believe what He says!

If you doubt that what you believe could prevent God from reaching you then remember when Jesus was alive on Earth in His own Earth-suit as the son of Mary and Joseph. At times He was prevented from working miracles because of people's lack of belief. This was reported in the following Scripture:

54 And when he came into his own country (where everyone knew His family), he taught them in their synagogue, and they were astonished, and said, Where did this man obtain wisdom, and these mighty works (miracles they had heard about)?
55 Is not this the carpenter's son? Is not his mother called Mary and his siblings, James, and Joses, and Simon, and Judas?
56 And his sisters, are they not all with us? (He is the

carpenter's son we all know) then where did this man obtain all this wisdom and power?
57 And they were offended by what they knew of Him. But Jesus said unto them, A prophet has honor everywhere, except in his own country, and in his own house.
58 And he did not do many mighty works there because of their unbelief (faithlessness).
Matthew 13:54-58

Faith is trust or confidence in someone or something. In the Scripture above we see that familiarity with Jesus and His family prevented people from believing He was more than just a man, and because they did not believe, "… He did not do many mighty works there…."

When your body dies, you must have faith (trust and confidence) in God's willingness and ability to cover you with righteousness, or your unbelief will blind you from His loving action. God's spirit calls you to believe, but He will not force you to believe.

So do not think the requirement that you believe in Jesus' sacrificial death is unfair. Rather, be thankful you can be cleaned up and covered with righteousness by simply believing this free gift from God. He has provided an easy way for you and me to be righteous before Him.

The message of this free gift is called the Gospel, or "good news". Jesus has commanded that we share this Gospel with everyone. He does not want anyone to perish. Don't make this complex; all He seeks is the faith of a child.

Look at what the Scripture says about this:

9 The Lord is not slack concerning his promise, as some men count slackness; but is patient with us, not willing that anybody should perish, but that all should come to repentance. 2 Peter 3:9

17 Therefore if any man be in Christ, he is a new creature: old things are passed away; behold all things are become new. 2 Corinthians 5:17

1 There is therefore now no condemnation to them which are in Christ Jesus, who walk not after the

flesh, but after the Spirit.
2 For the law of the Spirit of life in Christ Jesus has made me free from the law of sin and death.
Romans 8:1-2

5 Not by works of righteousness which we have done, but according to his mercy he saved us, by the washing of regeneration, and renewing of the Holy Ghost;
6 Which he shed on us abundantly through Jesus Christ our Savior;
7 That being justified by his grace, we should be made heirs according to the hope of eternal life.
Titus 3:5-7

8 For by grace are ye saved through faith; and that not of yourselves: it is the gift of God:
9 Not of works, lest any man should boast.
Ephesians 2:8-9

There you have it right from the Bible. "Grace" is the free and unmerited favor of God. "Faith" is the confident trust in God (believing Him). Pray that God will call you to faith in what Jesus has done. If you have trouble believing, then ask God to help you to believe. Yes, ask Him. He loves you and wants you to be in Heaven with Him.

Speak to Him out loud, he will hear you. Tell Him what you think of His free gift of righteousness given simply for repenting of our sins and accepting (believing) what Jesus has done. This is salvation by grace alone.

11 The Unforgivable Sin

You may have heard there is an "unforgivable sin", a sin so bad that God cannot forgive it. Wouldn't you like to know what that awful, unforgivable sin is so you can avoid doing it? It is quite simple. The "unforgivable sin" is to not believe what God has said about Jesus. There is no remedy for this sin because it is only the belief in what Jesus did for you that allows your sin to be removed. If you refuse to believe what God said, there's no hope for you. Not even God can save you. His edict is as fixed and as strong as the law of gravity. You have been given this knowledge, and if you choose to step off the edge of that cliff above the lake of fire that destroys corrupt souls, no one can save you.

God wants you to be at peace with Him so that love between you two can flourish. That can't happen if you hang on to worry about whether or not a sin has been forgiven. Turn from your sins and believe God.

> **18 Come now, and let us reason together, said God: even though your sins be as scarlet (bloody awful), they shall be as white as snow (cleaned up); though they be red like crimson (a bloody awful, stinking mess), they shall be as white as wool (no longer there as God sees you).**
> **19 If you are willing and obedient to the will of God (believe Him), you shall eat the good of the land:**
> **20 But if you refuse and rebel against God (disbelieve Him), you shall be destroyed; for the mouth of God has said this.**
>
> **Isaiah 1:18-20**

Be obedient to God by believing what He says. Repenting of your sins and believing what God said about Jesus gives you the Very Important Personality Characteristic of Righteousness. The righteousness of Jesus Christ that you accept by faith, by choosing to believe God, covers all your sins. You then become a refreshing, clean drink of water perfectly suited to God's heavenly places. Your life will be a pleasing fragrance to Him and He will desire to be near you.

If you do not believe what God said about Jesus, then you are "lost". This is not a good place to be. What other hopes could you possibly have other than the fanciful imaginations and deceptive philosophies of mankind?

12 What does it Mean to be "Born Again"?

The phrase "born again" comes from a conversation Jesus had with Nicodemus, a Pharisee with an open mind. He was curious about what Jesus was teaching and the many miracles he had heard that Jesus did. Apparently he was uncomfortable with his fellow Pharisees knowing of his interest in Jesus, so he arranged to meet with Jesus in secret. Consider this important exchange between Jesus and Nicodemus:

> **1 There was a man of the Pharisees, named Nicodemus, a ruler of the Jews:**
> **2 He came to Jesus by night, and said to Him, "Rabbi, we know that you're a teacher sent by God because no ordinary human being could do the miracles that you do, unless God is with him."**
> **3 Jesus answered "With utmost truthfulness I say to you, <u>a man has to be born again</u> in order to be able to see the kingdom of God."**
> **4 Nicodemus said "How can a man be born when he is old? Can he reenter his mother's womb, and then be born a second time?"**
> **5 Jesus answered, "With utmost truthfulness I say to you that unless a man is born of water and of the Spirit, he cannot enter into the kingdom of God.**
> **6 That which is born of the flesh is flesh; and that which is born of the Spirit is spirit.**
> **7 Marvel not that I said to you that you must be born again. (Second birth)**
> **8 The wind blows where it wishes, and you hear the sound of it blowing, but you can't tell where it comes from, and where it goes to: so is everyone that is born of the Spirit."**
> **9 Nicodemus said "How can these things be?"**
> **10 Jesus then said "Aren't you a master of Israel, and you don't know these things?**

11 With utmost truthfulness I am telling you that I speak what I do know, and tell you that I have actually seen this; and yet you don't believe me.
12 If I have told you earthly things, and you don't believe me, how then can you believe me if I tell you of heavenly things?"

John 3:1-12

In the passage above, Jesus clearly speaks about the first and second birth. He refers to the first birth as the birth of "water," which is a human body being born from its mother's womb. He also refers to the second birth, which He calls being "born of the Spirit," thus the phrase "born of water and the Spirit." He also clearly says if your spirit is not "born again" you cannot see the kingdom of God.

How do we become born again?

Being born again is not something a person does; it is something they experience due to an act of God. Jesus said it like this...

44 No man can come to me, except the Father which hath sent me draw him: and I will raise him up at the last day.

John 6:44

Clearly, being born again is an act of God. He draws any human spirit to Him which He desires for His Kingdom. To be born again means God has called you to believe what He says about Jesus, and thereby come to a relationship with God as a loving Father and friend. "It refers to a change of heart - from indifference or hostility toward God to a love for Him and a desire to live out His best for us."[25]

Jesus also said...

7 Marvel not that I said to you that you must be born again. (Second birth)

[25] PeaceWithGod.net, Billy Graham Evangelistic Association, "What Does it Mean to be Born Again?"

8 The wind blows where it wishes, and you hear the sound of it blowing, but you can't tell where it comes from, and where it goes to: so is everyone that is born of the Spirit." John 3:7-8

What he is saying here is that just as you cannot see where the wind comes from or goes, you can see its effect (such as moving branches in a tree). Likewise, the Spirit of God cannot be seen coming and going, but you can observe the effect of his work.

Some experience Him as a still, small voice deep in their heart of hearts. Learn to listen for that voice and receive it. If you hear nothing, then pray to God. Tell Him you are interested in Him and in being among His chosen people. Don't stop asking until you hear from Him.

Your liberation from your body (which occurs at the time of your body's death) will release your spirit into a very different world.

You do not have to wait for your body to die to be born again. This is because when He calls you, and you repent and accept His free gift of salvation, God covers you with Holy Spirit. Then when God looks at you He sees Christ's righteousness. You are a new creature from that moment on, and part of what you receive, if you will allow it, is the presence of Christ's spirit within you to give you the power to overcome sin. You can then begin to resist sin and improve your moral and personality characteristics, with God's help, to more closely match His own character. Receiving Christ's Holy Spirit, being born again, is the second birth, the birth by spirit. Here is how this gift is described in the Old Testament.

26 A new heart also will I give you, and a new spirit will I put within you: and I will take away the stony heart out of your flesh, and I will give you a heart of flesh.
27 And I will put my spirit within you, and cause you to walk in my statutes, and you shall keep My judgments, and do them.

Ezekiel 36:26-27

This passage in Ezekiel clearly presents the idea that God wants us to walk in His statutes, to keep His judgments, and to do them (obey Him). If God has never put His "new spirit" within us, if He has not given us a "heart of flesh," it will be impossible for us to obey God or even want to obey God. This is because even though we are spirit, we are dead to God spiritually. We have not been born again.

But if we undergo the second birth, the birth of our spirit into the life and knowledge of God, then when our Earth-suit dies we will arrive into the continued-life place covered with Christ's righteousness. We will be sinless, fresh and clean, perfectly acceptable to our Heavenly Father. The angels will come and escort us to the dwelling places Jesus has gone forward to prepare for us all. And our Father God has done it all. Our part is to be thankful and enjoy Him.

> **22 ... Lord, how is it that you will manifest yourself to us, and not to the world?**
> **23 Jesus answered, if a person loves me, they will attend to my words carefully: and my Father will love them, and we will come to them, and make our abode (staying, abiding, dwelling) with them.**
> **John 14;22-23**

This is exciting news. God wants to be close to us, and it's okay. First, we can trust Him because He is perfectly good. Second, he will not harm us in any way. After all, He created us to be in fellowship with Him. Third, He can dwell with us as a helper and one who loves us. This is not about God controlling us. This is about fellowship with One in who we are already in friendly (agreeable) relationship. *Relating to God with love and trust is the way it was supposed to be from the beginning of time.*

When His spirit knocks on the door to your heart, invite him to be a part of your day-to-day life. He will love that, and you will be blessed.

Some may ask "what happens to the spirit-persons in baby bodies that perish in the womb, or die after birth before they reach the age of accountability?" Are they "lost" to God because they never had a chance to hear that the Lord Jesus died for them? Are they lost because they did not have a chance to believe? The answer is that these very young people are called *Innocents*, and they are persons who have not yet rebelled against

God or sinned by disbelief. We can be sure that God will deal with these *Innocents* with wisdom and love. We can take comfort in remembering that the Creator is the one who has said that *He is not willing that any should perish.* Also, we read in the stories of people who have seen Heaven and come back to life on Earth that there are children in Heaven. So let your heart rest on this, that Father God loves babies and children, and would even go so far as coming down out of Heaven to enter a human body and die on the cross for them. So trust Him with them. Their spirits are more than okay.

In Rev 3:20 Jesus said,

Behold, I stand at the door, and knock:
if any person[26] hear my voice, and open the door,
I will come in to him,
and will sup with him, and he with me.

[26] The King James text uses "man" as in "If any man hears my voice…". "Man" was translated from the Greek word τὶς which means "some" or "any person". The Bible sees both males and females as "man" (mankind). See Genesis 1:27

13 When you hear the Call

Would you like your sin to be covered by the righteousness of Christ Jesus?

If you desire to know God and to follow in His ways, <u>you have been called by God</u>. A dead spirit would not be seeking God. This means the Creator of the entire universe has chosen you to be one of His children. This is obvious because you are not dead to God and have already begun to seek Him. The next step is to say a heartfelt prayer to God accepting His free gift of forgiveness. Something like this:

> Father God, thank you for creating me, and thank you for giving me the free gift of your son Jesus dying on a cross for the forgiveness of my sins. I repent of my sins. Jesus, I believe you died for me, and I thank you that all my sins are forgiven through what you did for me.

That's it. If you believe and say a prayer like that in sincerity, you have acknowledged that you are His child and are forgiven. You will be seen in Heaven with the righteousness of Jesus Christ. You have undergone the second birth. (Your spirit is spiritually alive to God!)[27] Your spirit, the real you, will be alive forever starting right then.

> **24 I say unto you truthfully, He that hears my word, and believes in God Who sent me, <u>has everlasting life</u>, and shall not come into condemnation; but is passed from death unto life.**
>
> **John 5:24**

Now that you will live forever, can you run off and do all the sinful things you want to do? Of course not, you are a new person in Christ, a child of the living God, *and you should act like it to the best of your ability.*

---

[27] Should you feel something when this happens? Individual experiences differ. Some people feel nothing, but begin to see changes in their lives in the days, weeks, and months that follow, such as more strength to resist sin. Some people experience a warmth flow through them, or the sensation of electricity flowing into them. Some are given the gift of tongues. Don't be disappointed; just trust God, accept what He lets you experience, and be thankful.

1 Having therefore these promises, dearly beloved, let us cleanse ourselves from all filthiness of the flesh and spirit, perfecting holiness in the reverence of God.

2 Corinthians 7:1

11 Knowing how short the time is to awaken from our sleep of ignorance; for now salvation is nearer to us than we believed.
12 The time of darkness is almost gone, and the day is near. Therefore let us lay aside the deeds of darkness and put on the armor of light.
13 Let us behave properly as in the daylight, not in carousing and drunkenness, not in sexual promiscuity and sensuality, not in strife and jealousy.
14 But make Lord Jesus Christ central to our life, and make no provision for the flesh in regard to its lusts.

Romans 13:11-14

21 If you've heard of Jesus and have been taught by Him, as the truth is in Jesus:
22 then you should put off conversations with your old self, which is corrupt according to the deceitful lusts;
23 And be renewed in the spirit of your mind;
24 And that you should put on the new man, which is created in righteousness and true holiness to be like God's personality.

Ephesians 4:21-24

His Spirit will give you the power to resist temptation and sin. Ask for that help, and obey Jesus' teachings and commandments to the best of your ability. Start reading the Bible. Ask Him to show you where you should start reading. Join a congregation of fellow believers and begin learning all you can about God and what He wants from His people.

What if you slip up and sin? We all do. Are you doomed to Hell? No, certainly not, because you are now a child of the living God who died for you. Satan's henchmen may come and tell you that you have fallen back under his power, but don't believe it (Jesus said Satan is the father of lies). Just pray to Jesus, admit your sin, and ask forgiveness in order to return into right standing with Him. Seek ways to make right any hurts you have done to other people and don't repeat those sins. *God loves to see His children behaving this way.*

> **9 If we confess our sins, he is faithful and just to forgive us our sins, and to cleanse us from all unrighteousness. 1 John 1:9**

If you felt the call and made a decision to follow Jesus, tell someone who can help you grow in faith.

> **32 Whosoever therefore shall confess me before men, him will I confess also before my Father which is in heaven. Matthew 10:32**

God wants you to know Him, enjoy Him, and love Him forever.

This is why you exist and why You are alive on Earth!

14 They Died and Returned to Life

Okay, so now you know who you are, where you are, why you are here, and where you are going. You know that the one and only loving God created you. He has provided a way for you to avoid the terrible trap of sin and the second death in the destructive fires of Hades.

Wisely, He does not require you to perform in some way to qualify to be in Heaven. This means He does not require you to make a pilgrimage to some far-off place, give a certain amount of money, walk up a mountain on your elbows, or any other challenge to prove you are worthy of Heaven. Your worthiness for Heaven comes from the fact that your Heavenly Father made you for Himself and for His Heaven. He made a way for you to reach Heaven through Jesus Christ, and ***you are supposed to be there***.

It does not matter at all what other people say about you in this regard, or how they treat you. Your worth and your value are not determined by people. God said you are of high value to Him when He made you in the first place. Besides, if we all had to perform a certain way to get to Heaven, then when we got there we would all be boasting about who was the greatest. We would hear things like…

"I'm better than you because I gave $50,000 to the poor."

"No, I am greater than you because I gave $75,000 to the hospital."

"No, I am greater than you both because I walked a mile on my knees and elbows to deliver a loaf of bread to a starving widow."

We can put all that nonsense aside because we all owe everything to Jesus. We can only confess "I am in Heaven because of the willingness of Jesus Christ to suffer for the forgiveness of my sins." Because eternal life is the free gift of God, none of us may boast about it. None of us deserve it, for we all sin. When we get to Heaven, instead of boasting, we can just be thankful that our Savior Jesus took our sins upon Him and cloaked us with His righteousness.

You might be curious what it's like for your body to die and your spirit to disconnect from it. The Bible has recorded several instances of this, such as the story of Lazarus, but in these cases no record was made of what the person who returned to life saw while his or her spirit was no longer connected to his or her body. We know, however, that some people have died and then come back to life, and sometimes those people are able to remember what happened to them after death.

Some have suggested this phenomenon is just dreams or hallucinations. But at times someone will come back to life and have information he or she could not possibly know. This is a confirmation that such after-death experiences are real, and not just figments of the person's imagination. You can see an example of this confirmation of some impossible-to-be-known facts in the story of Colton Burpo (referenced below).

You are encouraged to use the names below to view the YouTube testimonies of several people who died and whom God allowed to return to life. Just enter the person's name in the YouTube search line and then the word "testimony." You could also search for "life after death experiences" with the person's name.

1. **The Ian McCormack testimony** – A young man who was not a strong believer in Jesus Christ was in a hospital emergency room, dying from poisonous stings he had received from a box jellyfish while swimming in the ocean. He eventually came back to life on Earth after speaking with God and now travels around the world telling his amazing story. You can hear him tell it by searching for "A Glimpse of Eternity" (Ian McCormack, Jellyfish Man).

2. **Angie Fenimore testimony** – Angie was a young mother who successfully suicided on an overdose of pills. In Angie's testimony we see evidence of the great love of God. He really cares for people and will even redeem those who have made major errors in their lives. This young mother does not talk directly about her faith in Christ, but you can tell from her comments that she knew the story of Christ's life and death on the cross. Remember 2 Peter 3:9 says, "The Lord is ... not willing that any should perish, but that all should come to repentance."

3. **Tamara Laroux testimony** – This lady shot herself, went to Hell, then to Heaven, and was returned to Earth by our Lord. Her description of Hell in her book *Delivered – A Death-Defying Journey into Heaven and Hell* contains one of the clearest descriptions of what being in Hell is like.

4. **Dean Braxton testimony** – Mr. Braxton died while under intense medical care and saw Heaven. Be sure to listen to the discussion portion after the first session.

5. **Darnisha Taylor testimony** – A young woman scuba diving with her husband encountered equipment failures that resulted in her drowning. In her spirit she saw the new world, at least a glimpse of it, and communicated with someone she encountered there.

The next testimony (Howard Storm) demonstrates that even if at some time in our lives we did believe, that might be enough to save us. We know God the Father saves people even at the last instant. Just remember the thief on the cross who pleaded with Christ to be in His kingdom just before he died, and Jesus granted it to him.

6. **Howard Storm testimony** – Watch Howard Storm's testimony. He died while lying on a bed with his wife nearby. He needed an operation to save his life, but there was no doctor available.

7. **Mickey Robinson testimony** – Injured in an airplane crash, this man saw things after death that you might be interested in knowing about.

8. **Bryan Melvin testimony** – A young construction worker died and returned with what he saw.

9. **Colton Burpo story** – A young boy had a Heavenly experience and proved he really did see Heaven by revealing information he could not possibly know.

10. **Jim Woodford (interview with Sid Roth)** – Jim Woodford was brain dead for eleven hours after an accidental overdose of his prescription medications. He was suffering from Guillain-Barré Syndrome. He had an out-of-body experience and he was taken to Heaven. He went through a tunnel of light. He found himself standing on the edge of Heaven and a pit of utter darkness. Then a horrible creature in the pit called his name, climbed out of the pit, and …

11. **The Testimony of a Catholic lady named Pauline** – Killed in a bus accident, the Catholic Woman from Columbia dies, experiences demons and hell, is saved by Jesus to Heaven and then is sent back to earthly life to work on some issues. Jesus speaks to her about errors in her life related to the Catholic Church. If you are Catholic, be sure to watch this one.

One word of caution – there are many testimonies on the internet about life after death. These videos require you to trust and believe they are not just made-up stories. People can make money from YouTube videos, which provides the incentive to make up stories that become so popular that the video maker can sell ads or books. So watch with caution, and especially reject any such video that contradicts what the Holy Bible says or what Jesus teaches.

Now that you have a foundation of knowing who you really are and why you are alive on Earth, you should realize how much you are loved and wanted by God. He has a great future for you no matter your present circumstances. What does Jesus want you to do? We'll look at that in the next chapter.

15 Here is What God Expects You to Do

Assuming you accepted God's free gift of forgiveness though Jesus Christ, you are now more aware of who you are and why you have been given life. It would be natural for you to ask the question "What does God want me to do? What does He expect of me?" He has already answered these questions. Consider this offer from Jesus:

> 28 **Come to me, all of you who labor and are heavy laden, and I will give you rest.**
> 29 **Take my yoke upon you, and learn of me; for I am meek and lowly in heart: and ye shall find rest unto your souls.**
> 30 **For my yoke is easy, and my burden is light.**
> **Matthew 1:28-30**

He is using the imagery of His day when there were no machines to help the farmer prepare the fields or harvest the grain. Oxen were used to pull the plough or turn the threshing mill. The yoke was a wooden bar placed over the neck of a pair of animals so they could pull together. Jesus is saying you will find His lordship over your life "easy" and "light."

When He says "my yoke," He is telling you that He is already doing the work of God and is inviting you to pull together with Him. Please understand this does not mean <u>your life</u> will necessarily be easy. We live in a sinful, fallen world, and although God will no longer see your sins, you will not instantly act perfectly. You will need to work with Holy Spirit to correct your faults, and you will have to continue to deal with other sinners as long as you live on Earth. You may even suffer persecution from family, friends, neighbors, and religions which oppose the good news. But He will be there with you always.

> 28 **And we know that all things work together for good to them that love God, to them who are the called according to his purpose.**
> **Romans 8:28**

If you will look at the things God asks you to do while you are on Earth, you can see they are not heavy burdens. Do them as best you can, when you are able, and as your resources allow, and He will be pleased. (So many people totally ignore God; He will be very pleased to see you acknowledging Him and working on the list below.)

Do the following and you will do well.

1. Love God and love your neighbor as much as you love yourself.

> **28 And one of the scribes came, and having heard them reasoning together, and perceiving that he had answered them well, asked Him, Which is the first commandment of all?**
> **29 And Jesus answered him, The first of all the commandments is, Hear, O Israel; The Lord our God is one Lord:**
> **30 And you shalt love the Lord thy God with all your heart, and with all your soul, and with all your mind, and with all your strength: this is the first commandment.**
> **31 And the second (most important commandment) is this, you shall love your neighbor as yourself. There is no other commandment greater than these.**
> **Mark 12:28-31**

2. Care for widows and the fatherless, and keep yourself unspotted from the world.

> **27 Pure religion and undefiled before God and the Father is this, To visit the fatherless and widows in their affliction, and to keep himself unspotted from the world. James 1:27**

3. Forgive those who hurt or wrong you.

> **21 Then came Peter to Him, and said, Lord, how often shall my brother sin against me, and I forgive him? Seven times?**
>
> **22 Jesus said to him, I say not seven times: but, seventy times seven.**
>
> **Matthew 18:21-22**

To obtain a clear view of the importance Jesus places on forgiveness, read all of Matthew 18. Forgiveness is very important.

4. Give willingly.

> **38 Give, and it shall be given unto you; good measure, pressed down, and shaken together, and running over, shall men give into your bosom. For with the same measure that you give out shall be measured back to you again. Luke 6:38**

This giving does not necessarily mean to a church and it is not restricted to giving money. You can give your possessions, your time, your knowledge, your prayers, your skills, and anything else you can think of. Just listen to Father God and follow what He says. If you don't give, Father God will continue to love you. We do not give to others to earn God's love; we give because He is our example and gives His love to us without ceasing. Anything we do or give should be because we love Him, because He first loved us.

5. Rejoice! (Be happy!) Pray as the Spirit leads you, and give thanks to God in everything.

> **16 Rejoice evermore.**
> **17 Pray without ceasing.**
> **18 In everything give thanks: for this is the will of God in Christ Jesus concerning you.**
>
> **1 Thessalonians 5:16-18**

6. Read the New and Old Testament in the Bible remembering that obedience to God is important because His words and ways are good for you and can help protect you from the pitfalls of life. Search those words for commands or directions where you can practice obedience. For example,

> 18 **Flee from sexual immorality. All other sins a person commits are outside the body, but whoever sins sexually, sins against their own body.**
> 19 **Do you not know that your bodies are temples of the Holy Spirit, who is in you, whom you have received from God? You are not your own;**
> 20 **you were bought at a price. Therefore honor God with your bodies.** 1 Corinthians 6:18-20

This is the one sin God says "run from it". This is because it is too powerful for someone to try to think or argue their way out of. Turn and run. Sexual immorality has many forms…

Fornication: Sexual intercourse between people not married to each other.
Adultery : Voluntary sexual intercourse between a married person and a person who is not his or her spouse.
Prostitution: The practice or occupation of engaging in sexual activity with someone for payment.
Homosexuality: 1 Corinthians 6;9, 1 Timothy 1:10, Romans 1:29-31, and Leviticus 20:13

7. Tell others about what God has done for you.

What He has done for you is your "testimony". Share what you have learned about God and His marvelous free gift of eternal life with everyone you know.

Do all the above and you will do well.

End

If you are in Christ, you are a new
creature: old things are passed
away; behold all things are become
new. 2 Corinthians 5:17

O death, where is your sting?
O grave, where is your victory?
1 Corinthians 15:55

Appendix A: Is Hell Real?

Many people have chosen not to believe in Hell. They often base this belief on the argument that a loving God would not send anybody there. But as you know after reading this book, He does not send anybody there anymore than He causes you to be killed if you are careless enough to step off a 1,000-foot cliff here on Earth. You bring the end of you upon yourself by the choices you make. You choose the path on which to place your feet; slippery or firm. But do not doubt that Hell is real. Jesus spoke of it.

> **41 The Son of man shall send forth his angels, and they shall gather out of his kingdom all things that offend, and them which do iniquity;**
> **42 And shall cast them into a furnace of fire: there shall be wailing and gnashing of teeth.**
> ...
> **49 So shall it be at the end of the world: the angels shall come forth, and sever the wicked from among the just,**
> **50 And shall cast them into the furnace of fire: there shall be wailing and gnashing of teeth.**
> **Matthew 13:41-42, 49-50**

> **22 "But I say to you that everyone who is angry with his brother shall be guilty before the court; and whoever says to his brother, 'You good-for-nothing,' shall be guilty before the supreme court; and whoever says, 'You fool,' shall be guilty enough to go into the fiery hell." Matthew 5:22**

God has allowed some people to go to Hell and come back and tell us what it's like. You are encouraged to Google YouTube for "In Hell" and watch some of the true experiences folks have had. One of the most informative is **"The Bill Wiese story – 23 Minutes in Hell**." Mr. Wiese tells of his being sent there to be a witness to those of us still alive that Hell is very real.

End of Appendix A

Appendix B: Your Personality Improvement

That you even want God's personality pleases Father God. He cherishes those who seek His face, who long to be pleasing to Him. Consider these words:

> **1 The fool has said in his heart, There is no God. Corrupt are they, and have done abominable iniquity: there is none that does good.**
> **2 God looked down from heaven upon the children of men, to see if there were any that did understand, that did seek God.**
>
> **Psalm 53:1-2**

> **9 For the eyes of the Lord run to and fro throughout the whole Earth, to show Himself strong in the behalf of them whose heart is perfect[28] toward Him.**
>
> **2 Chronicles 16:9**

How to Improve your Personality in Preparation for Heaven

1) **Be in right standing**: The first step to obtaining a personality compatible with the Creator is to sincerely pray the prayer in Chapter 13. This puts you in right standing with God and cloaks you in the righteous mantle of Jesus Christ. You are then sinless before God and have access to Holy Spirit. Ask Him to dwell in you and help you obtain a personality compatible with God. (You have friends in high places.)

2) **Evaluate your life**: There are some practical things you can do to begin changing your old personality into a new personality. The first is to study the characteristics of God's personality one by one and do a serious evaluation of your life and interactions with others in light of these attributes. You will be strong in some and weaker in others, but the

---

[28] "Perfect" as used here from the Hebrew means "friendly" or "at peace with". You do not have to be faultless for God to love and seek you.

important thing is to be aware of them as you go through everyday life.

Here's a list of Godly attributes you can work on:

Be Just – In your interactions with others be fair to every person, and conform to the Law (The Ten Commandments) as best you can.

Be Good – Stop yourself from doing things that are wrong, especially evil things. Have no part in ungodliness in any form. This means you might want to consider who you hang out with, and avoid those whose lifestyles will bring you down. Keep away from lawlessness and sexual sin.

Be Merciful – Be willing to let go of the desire to punish those who have wronged you. [29]

Be Gracious – Be willing to give grace toward sins others commit against you. Remove the memory of those sins as far as the east is from the west (forget and never recall them). [30]

Be Longsuffering – Be patient, and be willing to wait, for yourself or for the benefit of another. Work on being slow to anger.

---

[29] Remember that there are sometimes criminal or civil crimes associated with wrongdoing. In these cases, the wrongdoings have consequences God has prepared the government to address. Thus if you have been raped, or beaten, or cheated out of money, for example, God does not prohibit you from seeking appropriate redress or compensation from, or prison time for, the perpetrator. But let go of your desire to punish and let God do the punishing via the law and legal consequences so that justice is done. Guard your heart. *Harboring unforgiveness will harm you if you cling to it.* Turn the perpetrator over to God.

[30] Ibid

Be Truthful – Tell the truth with meekness and gentleness in love, and make sure you are trustworthy in everything you say. Don't hide from God. Invite Him into your life every day, and confess any sins to Him. To do otherwise is to live a lie. *Invite Him to know your every thought.*[31]

Be Forgiving – Forgive everyone who has wronged you, or wrongs you in the future. Forgive yourself if you mess up.[32]

Be Wise – Focus on making good decisions using the information you have. Be willing to learn. Saturate your mind with truth from the Holy Bible. Learn to discern spirits. Fellowship with other believers.

Be Loving – In all your actions, care for others with agape love, the type of love that asks for nothing in return.

Be Gentle – Work on exhibiting a mild temperament or behavior, having a tender heart, and responding to the actions of others with kindness. Jesus is a gentle soul, and so should we all be.

Be Steadfast – Be consistent, trustworthy, not wishy-washy or changing all the time.

Be Able to be Righteously Angry – Allow anger only for right reasons such as in opposition to wickedness, evil deeds, evil plotting, hatred, and unforgiveness.

[31] Don't be afraid to let Him in on your thoughts. He is kind, gentle, and unobtrusive. He can help you resist sin. Besides, He already knows every single thing you have thought or done. Giving Him permission is just another way to draw close to Him, which He loves.

[32] See the previous footnote for being merciful.

Be Faithful – Live your life so people can truly say you are trustworthy in all things. Live so that others can count on you.

Be Righteous – Jesus has you covered on this one as far as how God sees you, but you can still work on it by trying to have no sin and never "missing the mark" (sinning). Work on this to the best of your ability.

3) **Take every thought captive**. Consider the following Scripture:

3 For though we walk in the flesh, we do not war in the ways of the flesh:
4 (For the weapons of our warfare are not carnal, but mighty through God to the pulling down of strong holds;)
5 Casting down imaginations, and every high thing that exalts itself against the knowledge of God, and bringing into captivity every thought to the obedience of Christ;

2 Corinthians 10:3-5

You have the ability to examine your thoughts before you speak them or act on them. Be slow to speak, give yourself time to think about what you're about to say or do, and then modify your words or actions to "bring them into captivity to the obedience of Christ." This means make your words or actions pleasing to Jesus.

An example of this would be when someone makes a nasty comment about you and your first reaction is to strike back at him or her with your words, perhaps to curse the person or unleash a nasty comment back in his or her direction. You must train yourself to stop and ask the question "Is what I'm about to say or do going to be pleasing to Jesus my Savior?" That habit of questioning your thoughts and actions before releasing them into action will give you time to think about what's happening and time to make the conscious decision to return good for evil, to be kind and not vengeful, to be gentle and not loud and belligerent. The Scripture says:

1 A soft answer deflects anger: but hurtful words stir up anger. Proverbs 15:1

4) **Pray for help**: Praying is just talking with God. You can do it in your head or with your voice; He hears both. Don't hesitate to talk to Him. You are His child. He is interested in your situation and well-being, and He will listen to you. You can ask Him anything such as "Lord, help me with my temper," or "Lord, help me control my mouth when I'm around Julia," or "Lord, please help me get my finances in order." Talk to Him as you would a kind, gentle, human father. If you are angry about something, tell Him. Remember, He too lived in a human body and is understanding and compassionate about our human conditions and weaknesses.

Part of praying is listening. God is said to have a "quiet, small voice," meaning He is not a shouter and you must listen closely. He may answer with words in your mind, an audible voice, words from wise fellow believers, or as you read Scripture the answer may be revealed to you. And sometimes He can say "no" to prayers such as "Lord, would you please give me a million dollars, a new, sports car, and a good-looking movie star to ride in a car with me?" Answer: "No!" or silence.

His answers will always be in your best interest. Compare what you think you hear God saying to what Scripture says, and get the opinion of fellow believers; to be sure you are hearing God before you act.

5) **Get control of your tongue.** Read James 3:1-12

Even so the tongue is a little member, and boasts great things. Behold, how great a conflagration a little fire kindles!
6 And the tongue is a fire, a world of iniquity: so is the tongue among our members, that it defiles the whole body, and sets on fire the course of nature; and it is set on fire of hell.

James 3:5-6

Words can be very damaging to relationships between people or between nations. Use the skill of taking every thought captive to assure that what you speak is good, true, and appropriate. Never use words to purposely hurt another person (who is also a child of the living God).

6) **Live your life for others**. Find a place of service where you can give your life to other people. This could be in your free time, in your vocation, or as part of a hobby or interest you have. Give your time, talents, and resources to others. You don't have to be a missionary to please God. Loving Him pleases Him. Just learn to love Him.

7.) **Be in regular fellowship** with other believers. They will help you grow and keep you from error.

8.) **Read and study the Holy Bible:** by yourself and in groups of people really interested in learning more about Jesus Christ and Holy Spirit.

End of Appendix B

Appendix C: Dealing with Others

Knowing Why You Are Alive Should Affect Your Behavior

Now that you know what you are, here is a new idea as to how you might want to conduct your life. Consider the importance of developing a personality (that spirit side of you) that honors all the other beings God has created and has placed around you.

Sometimes people grow older in their human bodies and never come to the knowledge that they are spirit beings and that everyone else around them is also a spirit being.

Since human bodies are not always formed perfectly. Some people end up in a human body that is deformed in some manner, such as being born without legs, being born without an arm, or being born with a DNA that calls for a less-than-beautiful face. Sometimes the DNA will cause us to grow fat, or sometimes human bodies become fat because of failing to eat properly and exercise. Sometimes the connections in the human brain are not made correctly or are damaged by disease or accident, resulting in a human body that cannot clearly speak or control its muscles in a normal manner.

You might treat those other people badly, cursing them, striking them, putting them down verbally, bullying them, or making fun of them. If so, remember that you are actually doing those things to a spirit-person, and soul that God values very much. This is something you should never do. If you do those kinds of things you will be at odds with God and sooner or later will have to face Him about your cruelty. Believe me; you do not want to be in that position. Behaving that way will open you up to satanic attack. Learn to love those who are less than perfect, not pretty, not handsome, or lack skills or even social graces.

Remember, you are not perfect, and that even in these bodies that are not so pretty, deep down inside is the person God has made, and that person is looking out of that body at you. If you make fun of that person, or tease that person for his or her disability or appearance, you are teasing or degrading the person God has made who inhabits that body. This is a person God loves and values very much. Someday after your body dies, you will come face-to-face with this person and God, and have to account for the way you treated him or her on Earth. This could be very difficult and embarrassing for you.

A better way of living, and a better personality for you, would be to treat all people with honor, for they are fearfully and wonderfully made spirits. Never malign (put down or pour scorn on) people for the shape of their bodies, their age, who their families are, their level of intelligence, the color of their skin, their sex, their race, or how they speak. You want to meet them in the continued-life and have them happily greet you as a fellow child of God who treated them well on Earth.

You are a spirit-child of God and are worth everything to Him. Behave like the child of the King that you are. Exhibit His personality characteristics to the best of your ability, and your Heavenly Father will be pleased with you.

End of Appendix C

Appendix D: Spirits, Demons, and Devils

Chapter 5 introduces the reader to the truth of the existence of devils and evil spirits. Since many people don't believe such beings exist, this Appendix was added to help overcome the narrow thinking that the only life on earth is physical life such as plants and animals. Remember, there was a time when people did not believe there were living creatures in drops of pond water. Mankind outgrew that false belief. Perhaps what is said below can help someone outgrow the illusion that evil spirits do not exist.

Consider this story from the author's childhood.

Across the street from his family home lived a man who suffered from stomach ulcers. For years, these ulcers put him in and out of the hospital, and many doctors were consulted. The remedies included anti-acids, drinking lots of milk, and, in worse cases, surgery to repair the holes being eaten into his stomach lining by stomach acid. Samples of the fluids in his stomach were sent to the best university research labs and everything looked normal. There were no disease organisms (biological "devils") found in his stomach.[33] Doctors were sure that the damage had to be due to the stomach acid that was eating the poor man's own stomach walls.

Flash forward many years and it was discovered that there actually were "devils" causing the erosion of the man's stomach; the bacterium Helicobacter pylori (H. pylori). It was there all the time. The problem was that science was blinded to it because the proper staining techniques had not been invented to allow this nasty bug to be seen under the microscope. This bug did not eat the walls of the stomach, but instead it interfered with the production of the mucus the body produces in the stomach to protect the stomach lining from its own acid.

Once the truth was believed, antibiotics were found that killed Helicobacter pylori. No pain, no gallons of milk, no surgery, just complete healing. The point here is that just because you can't see something does not mean it does not exist. This suggests those who follow only what secular science says might want to consider the possibility that you have not yet found the correct understanding ("staining techniques") that will

[33] The author is not saying germs are devils, instead he is comparing science's inability to see the stomach problem with the inability to see devils.

allow you to believe (and then see) that spirits, demons, and devils really do exist. Perhaps these examples will help.

Have you ever seen the wind? Do you believe that "wind" exists? Why? The truth is that you have never seen wind because air is transparent. You believe in wind because you have seen what it does: the bending of trees, the motion of wheat in a field, moving dust, or tumbling tumbleweed. You may have felt its touch on your skin. **You haven't seen wind, yet you believe it exists.**

Have you ever seen electricity? Do you believe that "electricity" exists? Why? The truth is you have never seen electricity because it consists of the motion of electrons which are too small to see. (Note that sparks are not electricity. Sparks are glowing gas heated by electricity.) You believe in electricity because you have seen electric motors move, lights glowing, stove burners become red hot, and sparks such as lightning. You may even have felt it flow through you when you touched an electric wire or walked across a carpet and then touched a doorknob or your sister's ear. **You haven't seen electricity, yet you believe it exists.**

These two examples demonstrate that the way to see invisible things is to look for the effects they create. If they are PHYSICAL invisible things, we look, feel, smell, hear, or taste their effects. Radio and television signals fall into this category. You can't see them, but you can detect them with the right equipment.

Evil spirits or devils are not physical, yet we can still see their effects if we look without our minds being blinded by the strong illusion that they do not exist. You need to know where to look. These beings act on the thoughts, affections, emotions, desires and imaginations of people, so it is in the behavior of people where you are most likely to see evidence of evil spirits. In Chapter 5 you saw examples of how these evil spirits express their invisible presence, and how they can be removed.

Fast forward to modern times and ask yourself what is going on when…

> Out of the blue, a loving husband murders his wife, four-year-old-son, and two year old daughter.

> A married man with children spends years of his life catching women unawares, brutally slaying them, and cutting up and burying the body parts.
>
> Jeffrey Lionel Dahmer, also known as the Milwaukee Cannibal, kills boys and eats parts of them and stores body parts in his refrigerator. Just crazy you say? He was determined to be legally sane at his trial.
>
> And consider the woman who put her little kids in the back of her car and then drove into the ocean to drown them?
>
> A mother found her naked boyfriend raping her 10-year-old-daughter and had to attack him with a knife to get him off of her.
>
> A woman withdraws under a crushing depression that came on her suddenly, and lived the rest of her life in a mental institution staring at the wall and nodding back and forth over and over again.
>
> Need we list the wickedly brutal ways Muslim ISIS members killed non-Muslim people, including little children?

Just calling such people "crazy" or "demented" is just modern science's way of saying "there is nothing in the stomach fluid." Is it possible that people trapped in the illusion that evil spirits do not exist just can't see what is really happening? Are they seeing the effects of invisible beings, and because of their lack of belief they invent other explanations?

So far science has been unable to cure the Jeffrey Dahmers or child molesters with anything biological or behavioral science can provide. Perhaps if they investigated the possibility of devils and evil spirits, new possibilities for real and permanent cures could be found.

One last thought on this subject. We know Jesus the man lived because there are historical writings about him. He claimed to be the incarnate God of the universe come to Earth in human flesh. Think about that claim, made by a man. You must realize that if he is not God then He was insane, deluded, or a liar. The odd thing is that he demonstrated that he could stop a storm on a lake by speaking to it. He could heal a man's arm that had been withered since birth. He healed a paralytic man, gave sight to a blind man, healed a woman with years of uncontrolled bleeding, and brought dead people back to life. He demonstrated that He could forgive sins, which only God could do. He also came back to life after the Romans killed Him by crucifixion and buried Him. He was seen alive by more than 500 people after his death and demonstrated the ability to pass through solid walls. And, to put the cherry on top of the sundae, He is still seen today by people all over the world (search YouTube for "visited by Jesus"). So the odds are pretty good that He is exactly who he said He is.

Remember, He spoke to devils, evil spirits, and demons as if they were real, and even drove them out of people, instantly curing them of their ailments. It should be obvious from this that spirits are real, even if you do not see them, because God demonstrated they exist.

It's a good thing scientists were able to finally see and believe in Helicobacter pylori or we would still have incurable peptic stomach ulcers today. How much longer will the human race have to suffer the attacks of these evil spirits before we lose our blindness, believe God's Word, and begin effectively fighting back. Think about that.

End of Appendix D

Dedication

This book is dedicated to the One Who makes each of us in secret, fabricated as in embroidering or needlework, in fine detail and rich complexity in the lowest (smallest) parts of the solid material (atoms) in our tiny body in our mother's womb. He is the One who took on human form in a baby at Migdal Eater thousands of years ago.[34]

Typical watch tower with manger below

[34] Migdal Eater means "tower of the flock". The place suspected to contain the manger in Bethlehem where the Savior was born. See Micah 4:8. Photo dated 1900 – 1920, source unknown.

Acknowledgements

Alice Bergan Blanchette, Piano Teacher and Author

1. I would like to acknowledge my Grandmother, Alice Blanchette, for her groundbreaking and creative work titled "Lessons in Personality Development for Boys and Girls", published by the Steck Company, Austin, Texas, in 1942. Her book led me to consider the growth of young people and the importance of self-worth in personality development.
2. I would also like to acknowledge my wife for her help reading and editing my work, providing that second set of eyes that catches the little goofs in the text my eyes can no longer see. Thank you for your patience sweetheart.
3. Thanks to my friend and bible scholar, Peter, who helped me understand some of the finer points of Scripture. Peter, your knowledge is amazing.

William Wordsworth, 1807, captured the essence of what happens to men and women after they are born here on earth.

Our birth is but a sleep and a forgetting:
The soul that rises with us, our life's star,
Hath had elsewhere its setting,
And Cometh from afar;
Not in entire forgetfulness,
And not in utter nakedness,
But trailing clouds of glory do we come
From God, who is our home:
Heaven lies about us in our infancy!
Shades of the prison-house begin to close
upon the growing boy,
But he beholds the light, and whence it flows,—
He sees it in his joy:
The youth, who daily farther from the east
Must travel, still is Nature's priest.
And by the vision splendid
Is on his way attended:
At length the man perceives it die away,
And fade into the light of common day.[35]

[35] From "Ode on Intimations of Immortality from Recollections of Early Childhood", by William Wordsworth, 1807. From The Norton Anthology of English Literature, Volume 2, First Edition, 1962 W. W. Norton & Company, INC.

What does Wordsworth's poem mean?

Scripture talks about God knowing us before we were born on Earth. Since being in the presence of God is glorious and a place of light, our leaving His presence and being born into the space-time continuum is like going to sleep and we forget where we were. The soul created within us, had its setting (end of day) elsewhere, and comes from afar (where God was).

But the soul has not forgotten everything and comes into Earth trailing the glory that surrounded it while it was with God. Thus heaven lies about us in our infancy. Earth is like a dark prison house compared to heaven, so the shadows of the prison house begin to close as the child grows. But he can still see glimpses of the light in his joy. He is moving from the east, the sunrise of his birth on Earth, a path he must travel. He in his youth is attended by the vision of Heaven, but eventually perceives it to die away, as the apparent realness of the physical world, the light of common day, causes the vision of heaven to fade.

This is the author's guess as to what Wordsworth was saying. The only part he was unable to understand was the line "still is Nature's Priest." If anyone has insight on this, zip the author an email to the address on the last page.

About the cover.

At the edges of the cover you see the deep-black darkness of nothing, where even empty space does not exist. It was from this God created everything. There is a glowing blue box which has right angles, representing the three physical dimensions of the space-time continuum created by God. The white glow spiraling out of the top of the box indicates that God's power is very active within the blue box. Our Earth is inside the space-time continuum and from it, out of God's active power, a constant and huge number of completely different butterflies can be seen leaving the three dimensions of space-time. You can see them breaking free into where God dwells, to be with Him, to know Him, and to love Him forever. Each butterfly represents a person, a human spirit, having had a distinct experience on Earth and having obtained a unique personality. These are people God wants for His kingdom. These are flying free to become dwellers in His Heaven.

This is a picture of your journey, if only you will believe.

Final notes:

No animals living or dead were used to provide the eyeballs on the lady's legs. They are plastic eyeballs were purchased at a local department store.

The cat is Mufasa, also known as Moofy, Fuzzy Pants, Fluff Ball, Cat Brains, Dust Bunny, The Gray Ghost, Chief Sleeps-a-Lot and a dozen other names. Part Maine Coon Cat, he was tricked into posing for the photograph by a tiny bit of tuna.

Comments to the author may be sent to Areli@CFL.RR.COM.

This book is available from Amazon.com books and, if not found on the shelf, can be ordered from any decent bookstore.

ABOUT THE AUTHOR

V. G. Blanchette is a graduate of the University of Alabama (B.S. – Physics/Mathematics) and the University of Texas at Austin (M.Ed.). He has taught in public schools, community colleges, and for General Electric Company in the commercial nuclear power industry. He recently retired as an engineer with URS Corporation at the Kennedy Space Center.

Mr. Blanchette, married with six adult children, has been writing for over thirty years, and is an alumnus of the Christian Writer's Conference at Lake Yale, Florida. His other published works include the two volume *Nuclear Terror Survival Handbook – Part 1 (Within one mile)* and *Part 2 (Beyond one mile)*; *Jehanne & Olivier* – a Love Story; *An Encounter with the Honey Island Swamp Monster* - a true but odd tale of a strange encounter; *Bubble,* a science fiction story; and S*afe Schools Now, Arming America's Teachers,* begun October 6, 2011, after the Sandy Hook massacre and written to provide the solution to school mass shootings. A two part science fiction story called Kneldt's Fantasy is in the works.

www.ingramcontent.com/pod-product-compliance
Lightning Source LLC
Chambersburg PA
CBHW071007040426
42443CB00007B/697
* 9 7 8 0 6 9 2 8 0 0 4 4 7 *